Structural Exegesis for
New Testament Critics

Also by Daniel Patte

Discipleship according to the Sermon on the Mount

The Gospel according to Matthew

Structural Exegesis for New Testament Critics

by
Daniel Patte

Trinity Press International
Valley Forge, Pennsylvania

BS
2377.5
.P38
1996

In Memory of
John A. Hollar
January 2, 1942–October 20, 1989

Library of Congress Cataloging-in-Publication Data
Patte, Daniel.
Structural exegesis for New Testament critics / by Daniel Patte.
    p.   cm.
Originally published: Minneapolis : Fortress Press, 1990, in series: Guides to biblical scholarship. New Testament series.
Includes bibliographical references.
ISBN 1-56338-178-8 (pbk. : alk. paper)
    1. Bible. N.T.— Structuralist criticism. 2. Bible. N.T. Gospels—Criticism, interpretation, etc. I. Title.
[BS2377.5.P38   1996]
225.6'01—dc20   96-42565
                                                                CIP

Printed in the U.S.A.
05 04 03 02 01 00 99 98 97 96
10 9 8 7 6 5 4 3 2 1

Contents

Foreword

In the foreword to Daniel Patte's earlier *What Is Structural Exegesis?* I attempted in very broad terms to relate structural interpretation to the other primary modes of New Testament interpretation. I should like to do the same in this volume, which is not simply a revision of the earlier one but a reconceptualization of how to do structural exegesis. My orientation is the fruitful tension and cooperation between historical and literary methods.

Form criticism has been, to some extent, a literary discipline because it has been concerned with the formal patterns in the pericopes of the Gospels (or other New Testament literature). But I would judge that it has been more strongly historical than literary because of its interest in the *development* of a given unit or form, and in the influence of the setting in life on the origin and development of both the form and content of the units of the Gospel tradition.

Redaction criticism has likewise been both literary and historical, but again I would deem the historical concern to have been dominant (certainly in the "classical" redactional studies of the 1950s and 1960s), although in some quarters redaction criticism has increasingly manifested a more literary-critical approach. Redaction criticism is literary in its intention to observe and analyze how the final author of a Gospel (or other document) shaped and modified source materials (tradition) and put them together. How does the author give expression to the theological interpretation of Jesus through stylistic and compositional techniques? But redaction criticism is also fundamentally historical in nature because it separates tradition from the author's contribution—rather than looking at the text as a unified whole—and assesses the connections and tensions between the two; it investigates the historical relationship between author and the author's community and the history-of-thought relationships among the Gospels.

I believe that most form and redaction critics have operated, implicitly or explicitly, with the assumption that the language of their texts primarily exercised the referential function. The texts refer beyond themselves to events, situations, conflicts, ideas—and meaning is not really available apart from this reference. The more recent social historians and sociological exegetes of the New Testament make the same assumption about the referential function of the texts.

The kind of "literary" criticism that pursues the quest for sources behind the Gospels or other texts is really a type of historical criticism because it is concerned with the temporal process through which the Gospels came into existence. Aesthetic or formalistic literary criticism, however, sees its texts primarily exercising the poetic linguistic function, or at least throwing this function into relief. Language exercising the poetic function attracts attention intransitively to itself and does not refer it to some object beyond the text. Poetic language (using the term *poetic* broadly to include narrative and various kinds of imagistic language) is able to grasp attention in this way because the various linguistic elements are locked into each other centripetally so that attention does not escape easily to the outside. This internal organization makes the text an organic unity and gives it semiautonomy. The text is grasped as a whole as people read it, rather than as something to be analyzed (into tradition and redaction), and meaning is seen to be a function not of the relationship between text and historical setting but primarily of the union of form and content in the text itself. Form is not a separable container for the content but is itself the shaping or patterning of the content. All of this is to say that aesthetic literary criticism is concerned with the surface structure of the text, the manifest union of form and content.

Structural criticism is a mode of literary criticism, but its object is not primarily the surface structure of the text. It focuses rather on the relationship between the surface structure and the deep structures that lie implicitly or unconsciously beneath, around, or alongside of the text. Structural criticism wants to account for the larger implicit structure that in some way generates the text under consideration. How and to what extent does the given text manifest the reservoir of formal possibilities that belong to literature as such? There is a sense in which structural criticism is referential, but it does not derive the meaning of a text from its reference to something nonliterary, that is, something historical, sociological, or ideational. It discloses rather how the text refers to the reservoir of meaning possibilities envisioned by the text. I should like to add that all "structuralists" cannot be pressed into the same mold, and surely not all of them would agree with my brief formulation here.

As Patte emphasizes, historical and literary disciplines should not be thought of as mutually exclusive. Structuralism has taught us that the two must be kept distinct and unconfounded. This is because the meaning that an item has in its own meaning system (its synchronic connections) is not the same as the meaning it has as part of a historical process (its diachronic connections). For example, the prologue of the Gospel of John, which foregrounds the divine preexistence of Jesus, receives a part of its meaning from its *relationship* to the story of the foot washing, which belongs to the same larger narrative. But in the history of christological thought, which we may see developing from one Gospel to another, the preexistence of Jesus is a *substitute* for the virgin birth and baptism of Jesus. The picture is further complicated by the fact that items that do or might belong to the same diachronic process may be *treated* synchronically, as related to each other in the same meaning system. But this carries us beyond the purposes of this brief foreword.

Deconstruction and reader-response criticism are the two developments in literary critical studies that have had the most provocative effect on biblical interpretation in the last decade. These two approaches often influence each other and are practiced together, but it is not too inaccurate to say that whereas deconstruction puts the emphasis on the slippery tendency of language itself to turn against itself, to fold in opposing thrusts that "deconstruct" any coherent center, reader-response criticism focuses on the creative role of the reader-interpreter in articulating the meaning of a text.

There was a discernible tendency in the structuralism of the 1960s and 1970s to understand the final goal of structuralist interpretation as clarifying the logical and abstract deep structure beneath the text. That is clearly not the final goal of Patte's present work. While he makes use of underlying structures, he employs them as a means for dealing with the surface structure, as a guide, in fact, for the close reading of the text. His method complements reader-response interpretation by focusing on explicit qualifications in the text rather than on the gaps in the text that the reader must fill in from his or her own standpoint. The question of the relationship of textual specifics to the construction achieved by the reader will be differently answered by different people. The very fact that Patte guides interpretation by means of a multiplicity of underlying structures indicates that his approach is not incompatible with certain aspects of the deconstructionist position; the multiplicity of structures generates the interplay of a multiplicity of potential meanings. Yet he would not want to say that there is no form or center to limit the absolutely free play of meanings, since for him structures are constraints upon meaning.

His book should be read with close attention to both the biblical text and the footnotes.

Dan O. Via
Duke Divinity School

ix

Acknowledgments

This book evolved in the classroom at Vanderbilt University, where I struggled to find an appropriate way to introduce my students— undergraduates, M.Div. students, and Ph.D. candidates—to the practice of structural exegesis. They patiently studied earlier versions of this book. This final version owes much to the several generations of students who, through their questions and comments, forced me to clarify and systematize the procedure.

Since this book and the computer-assisted lessons were prepared concurrently, the book owes much to the insights, pedagogical acumen, and critical comments of the Ph.D. candidates who helped me prepare the computer lessons: Timothy Cargal, Martin McDaniel, Robin Mattison, Vicki Phillips, and Jeff Tucker.

The critical comments of Dan Via, editor of the Guides to Biblical Scholarship, helped me further to clarify several important points and to correct outright errors.

Finally, the style of this book owes much to the relentless editing work of Pat Mundy, secretary of the Department of Religious Studies, and to the invaluable guidance of John A. Hollar, Editorial Director, Fortress Press books.

My thanks to each of them, as well as to Jacque Voegeli, Dean of the College of Arts and Science, and Russell Hamilton, Dean of the Graduate School, of Vanderbilt University, who provided the funding that gave me time to write this book and provided the assistance necessary to develop the computer-assisted lessons.

Introduction

This book introduces structural exegesis through a series of examples. Part One is an initiation to structural exegesis. Rather than providing detailed theoretical explanations that necessarily lead to the use of a technical vocabulary,[1] it explains each aspect of this methodology in the process of interpreting a text, John 3:1-21. Then, instead of general statements regarding the results that one can expect from a structural exegesis,[2] the second part of this book proposes the study of other texts (John 4:4-42 and Luke 10:21-42). A comparison of the results of the structural exegesis of these passages readily shows the contributions that this methodology makes to New Testament critical studies.

Such an inductive and concrete presentation of an exegetical method makes pedagogical sense; the best way to teach a method is to show how it is practiced. Yet in the case of structural exegesis, this mode of presentation is particularly difficult to implement. There are two related problems:

First, structural exegesis is deliberately derived from theoretical considerations. Consequently, one cannot present structural exegesis without discussing at least some of its theoretical basis. The challenge is to clarify

---

1. One can reach sound exegetical results by using the method presented in this introductory book; that is, without a detailed understanding of the theoretical basis of structural exegesis. But, to make a more sophisticated use of this exegetical method, and to understand how it is related to other exegetical methods (including historical-critical and literary methods), one needs a clear understanding of the semiotic theory upon which it is based. Daniel Patte, *The Religious Dimensions of Biblical Texts: Greimas's Structural Semiotics and Biblical Exegesis* (Society of Biblical Literature, Semeia Studies [Atlanta: Scholars Press, 1990]) introduces biblical scholars to structural exegesis by explaining in detail this semiotic theory.

2. As I did in chap. 1 of *What is Structural Exegesis?* (Philadelphia: Fortress Press, 1976).

the goals of structural exegesis while keeping the theoretical discussion to a minimum.

This problem is compounded by a second one: structural exegesis encompasses a series of exegetical methods based on different theories and involving quite different strategies for studying a text, even though they often have overlapping goals. Theoretical explanations seem to be required, to both justify each of these methods and show how they are interrelated. The challenge is to find a way of introducing the readers to a relatively wide spectrum of structural exegetical methods without multiplying the theoretical comments.

To overcome these two problems, we present structural exegesis as one six-step method. Each of the steps incorporates central features of one or several of the discrete structural exegetical methods mentioned above.[3] Consequently, the complementarity of these methods does not need to be argued in a theoretical discussion; it is demonstrated by using the six steps for the study of the same texts. Furthermore, since these discrete methods overlap, by presenting them as successive steps of a single method one can avoid repetitions. A given step focuses on central features of one or a few of these methods; other features are accounted for in other steps. Then it is possible to limit the explanation of these features to short methodological sections immediately followed by examples. In this way, with a minimum of theoretical discussion, the readers (1) are introduced to a broad range of structural exegetical methods (each of which can be pursued for its own sake with additional methodological studies suggested in notes and in the Annotated Select Bibliography), and (2) are provided with a multistep method that can be readily used by itself (without additional methodological studies) to reach significant exegetical results when studying any kind of biblical texts.

It would not have been possible to envision such an approach without the significant theoretical and methodological progress of the last twelve years.[4] I will now clarify how the six-step structural exegetical method proposed here[5] is related to earlier stages of structural exegetical research and to other exegetical methods.

3. For a select bibliography of works using these diverse methods, see the Annotated Select Bibliography.

4. That is, since the publication of *What is Structural Exegesis?* in 1976.

5. I used this six-step method for my systematic study of Matthew in *The Gospel According to Matthew: A Structural Commentary on Matthew's Faith* (Philadelphia: Fortress Press, 1987). Since the goal of this book was to present exegetical results, rather than to introduce the reader to a method, the six exegetical steps were not made explicit. Yet as soon as one is aware of these steps, one can easily recognize them in the treatment of each passage of the Gospel. In my *Paul's Faith and the Power of the Gospel: A Structural Introduction to the Pauline Letters* (Philadelphia: Fortress Press, 1983), I used a different strategy. Certain steps were used for the study of certain passages, while other steps were used for the study of other passages. Yet the six steps were used. Thus in these two books one can find many examples of the use of the method proposed here.

THE MULTIFOLD THEORETICAL BASIS
OF STRUCTURAL EXEGESIS
AND THE QUEST FOR META-THEORIES

The name "structural exegesis" was originally used to designate those exegetical methods deliberately derived from the theories of the linguist Ferdinand de Saussure,[6] and the anthropologist Claude Lévi-Strauss. As it came of age, structural exegesis became based on certain *semiotic* theories, the heirs of these pioneering theories. De Saussure's basic insights had been (1) that language is a system of signs, and (2) that signs are meaningful through their *interrelations* and their differences (thus, the concept of "structure"). Lévi-Strauss had then proposed that the principles that govern the production of meaning in language also govern meaningful social relations (such as kinship relations) and other cultural phenomena, such as myths. De Saussure's insights were developed by linguists such as Louis Hjelmslev, and Lévi-Strauss's proposal was applied to the study of any narrative, and then to a wide range of fields (such as literature, folklore, psychology, architecture, visual arts, as well as to the study of other cultural phenomena, including ideologies and sociological issues). In response to these developments, structural and semiotic theories multiplied and began to serve as the basis for a wide range of analytical methods used in biblical exegesis by themselves or in conjunction with other methods. The number of theories and methods multiplied as they moved further and further away from the proposals of de Saussure and Lévi-Strauss in the very process of refining these proposals and applying them to new fields. Conversely, general theories were progressively elaborated in an effort to understand the interrelations of the numerous discrete theories. These general theories are "meta-theories" in the sense that they aim at encompassing a series of discrete theories.

These semiotic theories can be classified in two groups, each giving priority to one of the two basic insights of de Saussure. One group of semiotic theories is primarily based upon de Saussure's insight that language is a system of *signs*; they take as their starting point the question of the process of communication by means of signs. Such are the semiotic theories of most North American semioticians. The corresponding meta-theories are found in the works of Charles S. Peirce or Umberto Eco. A second group of semiotic theories is primarily based upon de Saussure's insight that signs are meaningful through their interrelations and through their differences. When this insight is generalized, one can recognize that

---

6. For the works of all the scholars mentioned here, see the Annotated Select Bibliography.

in any meaningful phenomenon (including texts) meaning is produced through the interrelations, according to certain structures, of the features that can be perceived as different from each other. In continuity with Hjelmslev and Lévi-Strauss, such theories take as their starting point the question of the generation of meaning in and through any cultural phenomenon. Consequently, these latter theories are best designated as "structural semiotics." In his latest works, A. J. Greimas provides the meta-theory for this second group of semiotic theories; his general semiotic theory makes room for, and shows the interrelations of, a wide range of contributions in semiotic and literary theoretical research focused on the question of the generation of meaning.

THE MULTIPLICATION OF STRUCTURAL EXEGETICAL METHODS AND THE QUEST FOR THEIR INTERRELATIONS

Since exegesis aims at elucidating the meaning of texts, the semiotic theories focused on the question of meaning became the basis of structural exegesis. A diversity of exegetical methods was developed out of these diverse theories. Thus, certain exegetes[7] applied Lévi-Strauss's proposals to a study of texts of the Hebrew Bible and the New Testament. Similarly, Greimas's partial theories about narrativity (which progressively became more and more comprehensive) and didactic discourses (as a generalization of his narrative theory) were used in biblical exegesis. Other semiotic theories (including Barthes's and those of Russian scholars such as Bakhtin and Uspensky) are similarly used in exegesis, either directly for the study of narrative texts, or indirectly for the study of didactic discourses (such as Paul's letters).

The meta-theory, which Greimas recently proposed to show the interrelations of his own earlier partial theories with the various other semiotic theories that focused on the question of meaning, provided the basis for developing a six-step method of structural exegesis that would encompass major aspects of the diverse exegetical methodologies mentioned above. As this method is presented in the following chapters, we will mention in footnotes the relationship of each step with the exegetical methods mentioned above. Yet it should be clear that although these different methods are interrelated into a single six-step method, I do not want to deny that these methods should be pursued on their own terms. Indeed, we encourage the readers to do so, because these methods allow

---

7. For a list of the main applications of partial structural and semiotic theories in biblical studies, see the Annotated Select Bibliography.

the detailed study of specific dimensions of meaning in a text. Nevertheless, it is also important to provide an overall method that allows an exegete to deal in less detail with most of the main dimensions of meaning in a given passage.

Since the goal of this book is to introduce the reader to the practice of structural exegesis, in Part One a single passage, John 3:1-21 (Nicodemus), is studied in detail to serve as an example for the interpretation of similar texts. The process of interpretation is subdivided into six clearly defined steps. The methodological reasons for each of the procedures are explained as concretely as possible. Then, the procedure is implemented by reproducing the actual process of exegesis, including the hesitation one has when performing an exegesis, rather than being limited to those observations that will prove to be significant for the understanding of the text.[8] Part Two presents more rapidly the study of two other passages: John 4:4-42 and Luke 10:21-42. Here the focus is on the results of the exegesis. The study of John 4:4-42 will allow us to confirm our earlier suggestion that certain dimensions of meaning identified in our study of John 3:1-21 are indeed characteristic of the Gospel as a whole. Our study of Luke 10:21-42 will allow us to appreciate the results of the exegesis of the texts from John by showing how different are the results of the exegesis of a text from Luke. Yet these studies also have a methodological goal; they deal with different kinds of texts (an intricate dialogue in a narrative setting; a parable in its context) and are written in such a way that they might serve as exercises. Readers are invited to verify the proposed results by studying these passages more closely, following the steps described in Part One.[9]

8. A series of Computer Assisted Lessons that provide interactive initiation to this six-step exegetical method is available (see p. ii).
9. Computer Assisted Lessons that lead the user through the detailed study of John 4:4-42, John 10:1-18, Luke 24:1-53, Thomas 29–50, a section of the *Rule of the Community* of Qumran, and a passage of an early rabbinic text, the *Mekilta*, are also available (see this volume, p. ii).

PART ONE

INITIATION:
STRUCTURAL EXEGESIS
OF JOHN 3:1-21

1

Beginning a
Structural Exegesis
(Step 1)

METHODOLOGICAL CONSIDERATIONS:
THE NEED FOR
A COMPLETE DISCOURSE UNIT

The first step of any exegesis is to choose a passage from a text. While the "passage" must be chosen according to structural principles, the "text" (the Gospel of John) needs to be established before structural exegesis can begin. Thus structural exegesis needs to be preceded by textual criticism establishing the best manuscript evidence for the text, even though in the process of the exegesis one might be led to question some of the text-critical decisions. The text to be studied can be established in other ways, by reconstructing a given stage of redaction, or a source (such as the Sign Source).[1] Although structural exegesis is ill-equipped to participate in the identification of redactional stages and sources, it can study texts established in this way, provided that these texts are composed of complete discourse units. Yet since such redactional and source studies are done in order to elucidate the teaching of the text in its final form, structural exegesis usually chooses to study this final form. This is so because, unlike other kinds of exegesis, structural exegesis does not need to reconstruct the history of the text so as to elucidate central character-istics of the teaching of the text as a whole. This point is clarified as soon

---

1. Proposed by Rudolf Bultmann, *Das Evangelium des Johannes*, (Göttingen: Vanden-hoeck und Ruprecht, 1941, 1962), 68, *passim*. For a discussion of the many issues concerning redactions and sources of the Gospel according to John, see Raymond E. Brown, *The Gospel according to John. I-XII*, Anchor Bible (Garden City, N.Y.: Doubleday & Co., 1966), XXIV–XXXIV.

as we consider the structural principles to be used in the choice of a passage.

I have chosen to study a specific passage of the Gospel according to John: John 3:1-21. Why not 3:1-12? Or 3:1-15? Such a choice is never innocent; it predetermines the results the exegesis will reach. Consequently, this initial step should not be overlooked; it is quite important. In structural exegesis, the reasons and criteria used for selecting a passage and its limits are significantly different from those used in other types of exegesis. Structural exegesis has a different understanding of the relations between a text as a whole and one of its passages.

Two Views of the Relations between the Whole Text and Its Parts

Literary critics agree that one needs to interpret the whole in terms of its parts and the parts in terms of the whole in order to reach a full understanding of a text. The overall characteristics of the Gospel according to John are fully perceived only when the specific features of each of its passages have been elucidated. Conversely, the significance of these specific features is fully perceived only when one understands the overall characteristics of this Gospel.[2] It is clear that one cannot claim to have reached a full understanding of a text as long as these two interpretive moves have not been performed. The question is: Where should one begin? With the elucidation of the specific features of each of the passages? Or with the elucidation of overall characteristics of the text?

This twofold question is rarely raised because, for most exegetical methods, the answer is self-evident: one has no choice but to begin with the study of individual passages and their specific features. The characteristics of the text as a whole can only be established by drawing cumulative conclusions from the partial conclusions regarding the specificity of each passage. Yet by saying that this answer is self-evident, I suggest that it is a preunderstanding of these exegetical methods, rather than a tenet that has been critically examined. Structural exegesis questions this preunderstanding. While agreeing that, for practical reasons, one needs to study passages of reasonable length, structural exegesis claims that it is possible to begin *with the elucidation of certain characteristics of the overall text*, rather than beginning with the elucidation of the specific

---

2. For instance, Marxsen acknowledges this point in his comments about the Gospel according to John. He notes (1) that one cannot study the particulars of each passage (in his approach, through the study of the sources and successive redactions) without having studied the whole (through literary criticism), and (2) that one cannot study the whole (the final redaction) without having studied the particulars of each passage. "This is a vicious circle from which we cannot escape." W. Marxsen, *Introduction to the New Testament* (Philadelphia: Fortress Press, 1968).

features of the passages. This is so because, in itself, each passage reflects basic characteristics of the text as a whole.[3]

Criteria for Choosing a Passage

These two views lead exegetes to use quite different criteria for choosing a passage and its limits. For most exegetical methods, since the first task at hand is the elucidation of *specific features* of a passage (e.g., the use of a source or of a tradition, the historical situation to which it refers, its formal features, a theological point made by the redactor, a theme or teaching of this passage), the passage is limited to the verses necessary for the study of these features. Thus, for instance, if an exegesis aims at studying the meaning of "being born again/from above," then one chooses to study John 3:1-15, the dialogue in which this theme is included.[4] If an exegesis aims at studying the features of the historical narrative about Nicodemus (in contrast with those of the kerygmatic discourse of the evangelist), then one might want to limit the text to 3:1-12.[5] In brief, the types of features to be studied dictate the delimitation of the passage. By contrast, for structural exegesis, since the first task at hand is the elucidation of *characteristics of the text as a whole* reflected in a given passage, the criteria for selecting a passage and its limits are quite different.[6]

These criteria and the claim that one can and must elucidate certain characteristics of the text as a whole before elucidating the special features of a passage have the same basis: the semiotic theory from which structural exegesis is derived.[7] In brief, this theory describes the rules or structures

3. In methodological discussions, this point has been repeatedly expressed by emphasizing that structural studies are "synchronic": they study a text as a phenomenon taking place in a single time, the time of the discourse. See Daniel Patte, *What is Structural Exegesis?* (Philadelphia: Fortress Press, 1976), 14–20; Robert M. Polzin, *Biblical Structuralism: Method and Subjectivity in the Study of Ancient Texts*, Semeia Supplements (Philadelphia: Fortress Press, 1977), 14–18; Edgar McKnight, *Meaning in Texts: The Historical Shaping of a Narrative Hermeneutics* (Philadelphia: Fortress Press, 1978), esp. 93–143. Consequently, any passage is first studied as reflecting the whole of the discourse. By contrast, other methods can be called "diachronic," because they are primarily concerned with the succession of times. In this latter perspective, each passage is first studied on its own for its specific features and for its relationship with texts or traditions of other times, and the various passages are viewed as discrete times of the discourse.
4. This is the passage selected by Barnabas Lindars, *The Gospel of John*, New Century Bible Commentary (Grand Rapids: Wm. B. Eerdmans; London: Marshall, Morgan & Scott, 1972), 148–58.
5. This is the passage studied by Rudolf Schnackenburg, *The Gospel according to John* (New York: Seabury Press, 1980), 1:360–80.
6. This does not exclude the possibility that the passage selected might end up being the same as the one selected by another exegetical method.
7. I allude to the semiotic theory of A. J. Greimas, which is the most comprehensive theory. In this introduction to structural exegesis, I will evoke this theory only when it is strictly necessary, even though each aspect of the method of structural exegesis presented here is directly derived from it. For a systematic introduction to this theory, see Daniel Patte, *The Religious Dimensions of Biblical Texts: Greimas's Structural Semiotics and Biblical Exegesis* (Society of Biblical Literature, Semeia Studies [Atlanta: Scholars Press, 1990]).

that govern the generation of meaning in and through any text. With a knowledge of these rules or structures, in any given passage one can identify certain characteristics of the text as a whole—provided, of course, that this passage be properly delimited. One of these rules allows us to identify appropriate passages.

The Need for a Discourse Unit

A basic tenet of structural exegesis is that any text is a *discourse* that reflects a process of communication between an author and readers.[8] Other exegetical methods also recognize that a text is a discourse, and that understanding the text demands that the process of communication it reflects be elucidated. Thus, these methods proceed to a historical reconstruction of the author (the historical author) and of the situation in which he or she wrote the text, and to a historical reconstruction of the readers (the historical original readers) to whom the discourse was addressed, so as to assess the effect the discourse aimed at having on them. Yet, the main evidence for these reconstructions are found in the text itself. Structural exegesis (together with recent literary critical approaches) underscores that the evidence provided by the text needs to be interpreted with caution. The author does disclose himself or herself through the text-discourse, yet this self-presentation is at best quite selective, and often poorly reflects the distinctive features of the actual person who wrote the text. The author presents himself or herself as he or she would like to be perceived by the intended readers. Think about the different ways in which we present ourself when speaking to our parents, to our friends, to strangers, to a church, to a political gathering. Thus, structural exegesis emphasizes that, on the basis of the text (often the only available evidence in the case of ancient texts), the only "author" about whom one can really speak is "the author as inscribed in the text," often called the "implied author," or "enunciator," to avoid confusion with the historical person who wrote the text. Similar comments can be made regarding the readers addressed by the discourse and reflected in the text. These are "readers that the discourse envisions," often called the "implied reader," or the "enunciatee," to avoid confusion with the actual people to whom the text

---

8. This is particularly emphasized by the methods of structural exegesis based on the theory of Bakhtin, as in the work of Robert Polzin, *Moses and the Deuteronomist: A Literary Study of the Deuteronomic History* (New York: Seabury Press, 1980). Note that I refer to the process of communication inscribed in (represented by) the text, and not to actual processes of communication (when the text was read by its original recipients, or when it is read now).

was originally addressed, or with those who read the text at other times. [9] When we speak of the "author" it is a shorthand for "the implied author inscribed in the text"; similarly, the word "readers" is a shorthand for "the implied reader inscribed in the text."[10] Thus, when we said that "a text is a discourse that reflects a process of communication between an author and readers," we meant that it reflects the "ideal" process of communication (envisioned by the implied author) between the implied author and the implied reader.

This process of communication should not merely be conceived as the transmission of something (a message) to somebody, but rather as *producing an effect—a meaning-effect—upon the readers* (the implied reader). A discourse aims at transforming the views (or old knowledge) of readers. For this purpose, the discourse is necessarily organized in a certain way; it has a certain overall discursive structure that governs the interrelations of "discourse units" and "sub-units." The passages studied by structural exegesis must be complete discourse units or sub-units. [11]

Step 1: Identifying a Complete Discourse Unit

In order to learn how to identify discourse units, [12] we need to understand what this overall discursive structure is. It is enough to remember one of the basic rules of composition, the exercise of writing a good, convincing, discourse. A school paper, for instance, ought to have an introduction and a conclusion. The introduction formulates a problem

9. After the relationship between the implied author and the implied reader have been elucidated, the actual reading process can be adequately studied. Since this study (which can be envisioned on the basis of Greimas's structural semiotic theory) would deal with "hermeneutical" rather than "exegetical" issues, we do not discuss it in this book. See D. Patte, *Religious Dimensions of Biblical Texts*, chaps. 3–5.

10. The technical vocabulary is necessary in theoretical discussions aimed at establishing the basis for an exegetical method. But, in an initiation to structural exegesis such as this book, the essential is to propose methodological steps that make sure that, each time we consider the "author" or the "readers," we exclusively consider the "author as inscribed in the text" or the "readers as inscribed in the text."

11. As a consequence, the discourse units studied by structural exegesis are quite similar, and often identical, to those identified through a rhetorical analysis, i.e., a kind of analysis that also views the text as a discourse. The criteria used to identify discourse units in rhetorical criticism are quite similar to those proposed here. See George A. Kennedy, *New Testament Interpretation through Rhetorical Criticism* (Chapel Hill, N.C.: Univ. of North Carolina Press, 1984), 33–34.

12. The importance of this identification is emphasized by Louis Marin, *The Semiotics of the Passion Narrative: Topics and Figures*, trans. A. M. Johnson (Pittsburgh, Pa.: Pickwick Press, 1980); Group of Entrevernes, *Signs and Parables: Semiotics and Gospel Texts*, trans. G. Phillips (Pittsburgh: Pickwick Press, 1978); Jean Delorme, "L'intégration des petites unités littéraires dans l'évangile de Marc du point de vue de la sémiotique structurale," *New Testament Studies* 25 (1979): 469–91; and Jean-Claude Giroud, "Problèmes sémiotiques du découpage et des titres dans les traductions bibliques," *Sémiotique et Bible* 26 (1982): 10–24. As these works show, a text can be segmented into different kinds of units for different purposes. For our purpose, we seek the criteria that will allow us to identify *discourse* units.

or question which is the theme or topic of the paper. The conclusion restates this theme or topic, but now positively, that is, by expressing how this problem is resolved or how the question is to be answered. The body of the paper proposes the argument that establishes the validity of the conclusion. There are several conditions that must be met so that such a paper will be judged to be a good paper. Of course, the quality of the argument found in the body of the paper is quite important. But the introduction and the conclusion are even more important. If the introduction formulates a problem that, for the instructor, is a false problem, or a meaningless and absurd question, the conclusion will also be judged to be meaningless and absurd, whatever the quality of the argument. The student will receive a low grade.[13] As all students know, in order to have a high grade one needs to choose a paper topic (a problem, a question) that makes sense for the instructor.[14]

This is true of any argumentative discourse. The introduction states a *theme* in the form of a problem or question. The author usually presents himself or herself as being concerned by this problem; but, in fact, this problem is chosen and formulated because the author thinks it is *an issue in which the envisioned reader is interested.* In other words, in the introduction, the problem or question is formulated in terms of the envisioned reader's old knowledge. In an actual discourse (by contrast with the case of a paper exercise), the author anticipates that the reader does not know the proper answer to this question, or how the problematic situation described in the introduction is to be resolved. Consequently, through its description of the solution to the problem, the conclusion proposes a new knowledge to the reader, which is nothing else than the author's view of the issue. Thus the goal of the discourse is to transform the reader's old knowledge (an improper or problematic view of a theme, formulated in the introduction) into a new knowledge (a proper view of that theme, presented in the conclusion). We can say, therefore, that there is an *inverted parallelism* between the introduction and the conclusion. There is parallelism because both deal with the same theme; this parallelism is inverted because the introduction presents this theme as problematic, while the conclusion presents it as a resolved issue.

Inverted parallelisms between the introduction and the conclusion are found in any text-discourse, although they are expressed in many different ways according to the type of discourse (i.e., according to the

---

13. This is why, for such exercises, the instructor often formulates the problem (question) that is to be the topic of the paper.

14. That is, not merely, as students often believe, a topic that the instructor likes, but also and mainly, a topic that makes sense in the context of what is being studied in the course.

type of effect the discourse is expected to have upon readers). If an author aims at transforming the worldview, feelings, or general convictions of the readers, instead of transforming their knowledge about a specific issue, the discourse needs to be figurative. It might still have the form of an argumentative discourse, but it now includes metaphors and other figures of speech (as in the dialogue between Jesus and Nicodemus in John 3:1-21). It might be a poetic discourse (a poem). It might be a narrative discourse,[15] where characters and situations play the role of figures. In this latter case, it is easy to recognize the inverted parallelisms: the situation presented in the introduction is transformed by the time one reaches the conclusion. Thus, for instance, the Gospel of Luke is a narrative discourse which moves from the birth narrative (chaps. 1 and 2) to the resurrection narrative (chap. 24). A comparison of the beginning and end of this Gospel would allow us to identify inverted parallelisms (and thus transformations) between them. Then we could define the introduction and the conclusion as the passages that include these inverted parallelisms. The same applies to other types of discourses, although the inverted parallelisms between their introduction and conclusion might not be as easily perceived as in narrative discourses.

Inverted parallelisms also exist between the beginning and the end of each complete discourse unit or discourse sub-unit. This can readily be understood when one remembers another basic rule of composition. Each of the parts, and even each of the paragraphs, that form the body of the paper (as well as those that form the introduction and the conclusion) should have an organization similar to that of the overall paper-discourse. Each part must deal with a specific subtopic or subtheme that the author wants to communicate to the reader, and for this purpose this part or paragraph must have its own (mini-)introduction and (mini-)conclusion. The same is true of the discourse units and sub-units of any text-discourse, which can be identified by taking note of the changes in themes and of the inverted parallelisms that signal their respective introductions and conclusions.

These general principles provide us with two basic criteria for identifying discourse units in a text. (1) A *change of theme at the beginning and after the end of a passage* will be a strong indication that it is a complete discourse unit, since each unit has a specific theme. (2) *Inverted parallelisms between its introduction and conclusion* must exist before one can tentatively conclude that such a passage is a complete discourse

---

15. Note that rather than speaking of "narratives," I speak of "narrative discourses" so as to make clear that, from the perspective of structural exegesis, any narrative is viewed as a "discourse" addressed by an author (enunciator) to readers or hearers (enunciatees).

unit. This identification remains tentative until the theme of this unit is itself clearly elucidated—an elucidation that often cannot be achieved before performing other steps of the structural exegesis.[16] These basic criteria will be clarified by considering three examples.

EXEGETICAL EXAMPLE 1:
JOHN 4:4-42 AND JOHN 10:1-18
AS COMPLETE DISCOURSE (SUB-)UNITS

Before examining the Nicodemus passage (a more complex case), let us identify the discourse units (or sub-units) to which the passages about the Samaritan woman and the Good Shepherd belong. First, take note of the kind of discourse in which these passages are found. A glance at the Gospel of John is enough to recognize that this text is a narrative (since it presents the story of Jesus) that includes dialogues (as in John 3 and 4) as well as argumentative discourses (as in John 10).

In a *narrative*,[17] a change of theme is often a change of scene brought about by changes of character(s), space (location), and/or time. By locating such changes, one can easily identify narrative discourse units. Such is the case in the passage concerning the Samaritan woman in John 4. The story begins with a change of location expressed in 4:3-6: "Jesus left Judea . . . came to a city of Samaria, called Sychar . . . Jesus sat down beside the well." Since a new location is mentioned in 4:4, we can suspect that this verse is the beginning of a new narrative discourse unit. A new time is mentioned (4:6, "It was about the sixth hour"), and a new character is introduced, the "woman of Samaria" (4:7). In 4:43 we find a new change of time ("after two days"), a new change of location ("he departed to Galilee"), new characters ("Galileans," 4:45). These changes signal that a new section begins in 4:43. Since from 4:4 to 4:42 we find the interaction

16. The theme is studied in step 5. If step 5 shows that the identified inverted parallelisms do not correspond to the theme of the passage, we have to conclude that we have wrongly identified the discourse unit.

17. It is to be noted that, even in the case of narrative, we are not using the "narrative schema" as a model for segmentation in discourse units. For an example of the use of the narrative schema in biblical studies, see Jean Calloud, *Structural Analysis of Narrative: Temptation of Jesus in the Wilderness*, trans. D. Patte, Semeia Supplements (Philadelphia: Fortress Press, 1976). In brief, the narrative schema subdivides a narrative into three parts of the narrative development: (1) a situation of lack and the establishment of a qualified subject, (2) the decisive action(s), (3) a situation when the lack is overcome, and the retribution and recognition of the subjects take place. For the several possible formulations of this schema, see A. J. Greimas and J. Courtés, *Semiotics and Language: An Analytical Dictionary*, trans. L. Crist, D. Patte, et al. (Bloomington: Indiana University Press, 1982; French, 1978), 203–6. The narrative schema is not used here because it leads to the identification of "syntactic units" (units of the unfolding of a narrative), rather than "discourse units" (organized by the unfolding of a theme). Yet note that, in certain narrative discourses, syntactic units and discourse units are identical because the theme is exclusively narrative. "Discourse units" are what Greimas would call "units of the discoursive semantics."

of Jesus and his disciples with Samaritans in Samaria during a specified unit of time (two days, 4:40), it is fairly certain that 4:4-42 is a complete narrative discourse unit. Of course, this preliminary conclusion needs to be verified. A complete discourse unit has inverted parallelisms between its introduction and its conclusion: if we can identify such parallelisms and the theme they form, then we can conclude that these verses form a complete discourse unit. One can readily recognize one of the main inverted parallelisms that define its theme: at the beginning Jesus is separated from the Samaritans (cf. 4:4-9), while at the end the Samaritans come to Jesus and Jesus stays with them (cf. 4:40). This is enough to reach the tentative conclusion that 4:4-42 is a complete discourse unit—a conclusion that the other steps of the exegesis will confirm.

In contrast to narrative passages, in the case of *argumentative passages* the identification of discourse units or sub-units can only rely on more generally defined changes in topic and on inverted parallelisms. Such is the case of the passage about the Good Shepherd. In the midst of a discussion with the Jews about blindness and guilt (John 9:41) related to the healing of a blind man (a story that starts in 9:1), Jesus begins to speak about sheepfold, thief, and shepherd (10:1ff). In 10:16 Jesus still speaks about sheep, flock, and shepherd. But after 10:17-18, which explains 10:16, we find again the Jews discussing Jesus' healing of the blind man (10:19-21). From these observations, we can tentatively conclude that 10:1-18 is a complete discourse sub-unit, part of a larger unit that seems to go from 9:1 to 10:21 (as can be verified by using the criteria we used for isolating a discourse unit in John 4, since the beginning and end of 9:1—10:21 seem to be narrative). Of course, one still needs to verify that 10:1-18 is a complete discourse sub-unit by checking whether or not there are inverted parallelisms between its introduction and its conclusion and by elucidating its theme. Since we are dealing with an argumentative/ figurative discourse, we should expect that these inverted parallelisms and the theme they express are more abstract than in the case of narrative passages (where they often concern the relationship between characters, times, and spaces).[18] The procedure for identifying such inverted parallelisms and themes is illustrated by our next example.

EXEGETICAL EXAMPLE 2:
JOHN 3:1-21 AS A COMPLETE
DISCOURSE UNIT

In the case of the passage about Nicodemus we find a text with a mixture of narrative and argumentative features. First, note that in John

---

18. See the "introductory" Computer Assisted Lesson that deals with John 10:1-18.

3:1 a new character is introduced (a Pharisee "named Nicodemus"), and a specific time is mentioned ("by night"). Thus, we can suspect that a unit begins in 3:1. A study of what precedes confirms that 2:23-25 is the conclusion of a unit that begins in 1:43.[19] Similarly, in 3:22 we find the mention of another character (the collective character "disciples"), a new time ("after this"), and a new space ("the land of Judea"). We can conclude that another unit begins in 3:22.[20] Thus we can suspect that 3:1-21 is a discourse unit. But we cannot yet reach a definite conclusion. Although it is possible that these verses form a single unit, they might also include several discrete units.

This hesitation comes from the fact that the end of the story of Nicodemus is not clearly marked, as would be the case for a narrative discourse unit which, for instance, would end with his departure. There is no mention of Nicodemus after John 3:9, where he addresses a last question to Jesus. Furthermore, it is not clear where Jesus' answer to Nicodemus ends. After 3:12, the pronouns "I" and "you" that referred to Jesus and Nicodemus disappear. Could it be that 3:1-12 is a complete discourse unit? At first, this seems to be the case, since it is possible to find a number of inverted parallelisms between 3:1-2 and 3:10-12:

— In 3:1 Nicodemus is described as a "ruler of the Jews," and in 3:10 as a "teacher of Israel" who does not understand;[21]
— In 3:2 Jesus is designated as "teacher"; in 3:10 it is Nicodemus who receives this title;
— In 3:2 Nicodemus mentions what he has seen (the "signs that you do"), while 3:11 emphasizes that "we bear witness to what we have seen;"
— In 3:12 Jesus mentions what he has told Nicodemus (in 3:3), as well as other things he might tell him.

19. One can readily recognize the inverted parallelisms between 1:43-51 and 2:23-25. In 1:43-51, Nathanael believes in Jesus because Jesus "knew what was in him" (cf. 1:47 and 2:25) and what he did before their meeting (1:48), and Jesus "trusts himself" to him (cf. 2:25) since Nathanael will see the angels ascending and descending upon him (1:51). By contrast, in 2:23-25, people believe in Jesus, but not appropriately; Jesus knew what was in them, but here this knowledge has a negative connotation; Jesus does not trust himself to them. These inverted parallelisms confirm that 1:43—2:25 is a complete discursive unit. By these comments, I disagree with Brown who, on the basis of a single inverted parallelism with 3:18, suggests that 2:23-25 is the introduction of the Nicodemus scene. Cf. Brown, John I–XII, 126–27, 136–37.
20. This is confirmed by noting that later on we find the mention that Jesus "left Judea" (4:3), which suggests that this verse is the end of that unit. That 3:22—4:3 is a complete subunit can be verified by taking note of the inverted parallelisms between 3:22-23 (the mention that both Jesus and John baptized) and 4:1–3 (Jesus baptized more disciples than John, but it is not actually Jesus himself who baptized).
21. At this point we simply note that there is a difference between the two descriptions, although we cannot exactly say what this difference is.

These observations are important for our interpretation. Yet all they now mean is that 3:1-12 is part (the dialogue between Jesus and Nicodemus) of a longer discourse unit, *because there is no change in theme between 3:11-12 and 3:13-15.*[22] Even though the discourse is now in the third person,[23] the theme of 3:11-12 that emphasizes believing continues in 3:13-15 and in the following verses, as indicated by the fact that the lack of belief of Nicodemus (3:11-12) is contrasted with "whoever believes in [Jesus]" (3:15). The dialogue in itself (3:1-12) does not yet convey to the readers what John (the implied author) wants to convey about this theme. Thus the discourse unit is prolonged up to 3:21.[24]

The preceding observations show that it is highly probable that John 3:1-21 is a complete discourse unit. Yet this still needs to be confirmed. If there were no inverted parallelisms between its beginning and its end, then we would have to conclude that these verses are not a discourse unit, and therefore that we have overlooked another possible break in the text. In fact, such inverted parallelisms do exist and have already been noted by Raymond E. Brown, who calls them "inclusions":[25]

The whole discourse seems to be held together by an inclusion. The discourse begins with Nicodemus coming to Jesus at night; it ends on the theme that men have to leave the darkness and come to the light. Nicodemus opens the conversation by hailing Jesus as a *teacher* who has *come from God*; the last part of the discourse shows that Jesus is God's only Son (v. 16) whom God has sent into the world (17) as the light for the world (19).[26]

22. Unlike the case of John 10:1-18, 3:1-12 is not a complete discursive sub-unit of John's discourse (the Gospel), because here, despite the inverted parallelisms, the expression of the theme continues in the following verses.
23. The shifts from "direct discourse" to "third person discourse" can also be used for the segmentation of a text. See, e.g., Hugh White, "Direct and Third Person Discourse in the Narrative of the 'Fall,' " and John Dominic Crossan, "Felix Culpa and Foenix Culprit," *Semeia* 18 (1980): 91–96, 107–111. Such shifts express changes in the relations (distance, abolition of distance) between narrator and characters that represent changes in the relations of the implied author and implied reader with the discourse represented by the text. Yet in the same way that such changes occur within a discourse as a whole, they may occur in a discourse unit. Thus such shifts cannot be used to identify discourse units, although they must be accounted for in other steps of the exegesis (esp. step 6).
24. The continuation of the theme of 3:15 in 3:16 (cf. "believing," "eternal life") does not allow us to envision the possibility of a break between two discourse units at this point. Of course, this does not mean that one cannot perceive another kind of break here: for instance, a break between a statement (3:15) and its explanation (3:16-21). This is a reminder that structural exegesis does not deny that other kinds of units can be validly identified in a text; it is simply that structural exegesis needs to study discourse units in order to be in a position to elucidate certain characteristics of the Gospel as a whole.
25. The term "inclusion" used in rhetorical theory designates a phenomenon similar to that of "inverted parallelisms." The main difference is that rhetorical analysis tends to emphasize what is common to the beginning and end of a unit, while structural exegesis underscores *what is different* in the way in which the common theme is presented. Here, Brown also notes the differences. Cf. Brown, *John I–XII,* CXXXV.
26. Brown, *John I–XII,* 137.

To Brown's list of inverted parallelisms, we can add the more abstract contrasts between ideal actions described as "doing signs" in 3:2 and as "doing what is true" in 3:21; and between the conditions for these ideal actions—"unless God is with him" (3:2), "his deeds have been wrought in God" (3:21). We also note that 3:3 mentions "not being able to see the kingdom of God," while 3:19 mentions "judgment" (associated with being "condemned," 3:18, "perishing," not having eternal life, 3:16).

Although this tentative conclusion still needs to be confirmed by the elucidation of the theme of the passage (see steps 2 and 5), it is solid enough to proceed to the next steps of the exegesis. If John 3:1-21 is indeed a complete discourse unit, then we have a passage that can be studied in order to identify certain characteristics of the Gospel as a whole, as is explained in the following chapters.

CONCLUSION: THE THEME OF A RELIGIOUS DISCOURSE UNIT AS REFLECTING THE AUTHOR'S FAITH

The presence of these several inverted parallelisms confirms that John 3:1-21 is quite probably a complete discourse unit. Thus, as we suggested, John 3:1-21 should reflect basic characteristics of the entire Gospel according to John as discourse. What are these characteristics? How can we identify them?

Generally speaking, any discourse aims at transforming the readers'[27] old knowledge about something (deficient knowledge) into new knowledge, which is nothing else than the author's[28] point of view. Each complete discourse unit reflects basic characteristics of the process through which the readers' old knowledge is transformed; consequently, it also reflects characteristics of the author's point of view. In biblical studies these latter characteristics of the discourse are particularly interesting, since in the case of religious discourses, the author's point of view is nothing else than the *faith* that he or she strives to communicate to readers.

The *theme* of a unit, expressed in part by the inverted parallelisms between its introduction and conclusion, is one of the specific topics about which the readers' old knowledge is transformed into new knowledge. Following other exegetical methods, one can seek to identify the specificity of this topic as a step toward the understanding of the overall topic of the

27. More precisely, the "implied reader" (or enunciatee), that is, the "reader envisioned by the discourse represented by the text." Consequently, the readers' "old knowledge" is the knowledge that the text represents as being held by the implied reader.

28. More precisely, the implied author, that is, the author as he or she presents himself or herself in a specific discourse. The author's "point of view" is thus the view of the author as inscribed in the text.

Gospel viewed as the sum of its specific topics. From the perspective of structural exegesis, the theme of the unit also expresses basic characteristics of the Gospel as a whole, because it manifests the characteristic way in which the author interacts with readers. The theme of a unit is an example of the kinds of issues the author considers to be so important that it is worth attempting to transform the view of the readers toward it. These issues are important for the author, because they are related to his or her *system of convictions—his or her way of perceiving meaningful human experience* that establishes his or her identity as believer. This "way of perceiving," which is the same throughout a discourse, can be recognized whatever the specific topic of a discourse unit.

In the case of a *religious discourse* such as the Gospel of John, the theme of a discourse unit is most directly related to the author's system of convictions, or "way of perceiving human experience." Since a religious discourse aims at causing people to believe (cf. John 20:31), or at strengthening them in their faith, its goal is to convey to the readers certain of the author's convictions. More specifically, its goal is to bring the readers to share the author's way of perceiving human experience in the world and before God. Consequently, in such a case, the *theme of a discourse unit directly reflects basic characteristics of John's faith,* which, of course, pervades the entire Gospel.

It seems to follow from these observations that it is enough to study the inverted parallelisms that express the theme of John 3:1-21 (or any other unit) to reach important conclusions regarding the Gospel as a whole, and more specifically regarding John's faith. But the convictions expressed by the theme are not easy to identify, especially in the case of religious discourses, because they are expressed in terms of the views of the readers (as envisioned by the author). We shall discuss this further in steps 5 and 6 (chap. 3). Consequently, from the inverted parallelisms we can only deduce the main categories of convictions expressed by a discourse unit — yet the identification of these categories is quite significant, as we shall see in step 5.

As we consider the inverted parallelisms we found between John 3:1-3 and 3:18-21, it appears that two categories of convictions are underscored by the theme of John 3:1-21.

— Convictions about Jesus: he is to be viewed as the Son of God sent as the light of the world (3:18-21), rather than as a teacher who can be said to come from God because he performs signs (3:1-3).

— Convictions about people, and more specifically, about their responses to Jesus and the consequences of different kinds of responses: coming to the light, doing what is true and wrought in

God, having or not having eternal life, being condemned (3:18-21), rather than coming to Jesus at night, in darkness, not being able to see the kingdom (3:1-3).

In addition, we noted the inverted parallelisms between doing "what is true" and "wrought in God" (by would-be believers, 3:21) and "doing signs" because "God is with him" (3:2); these inverted parallelisms might be related to either of these categories of convictions.

This last comment, as well as the tentative character of our formulation of the two categories of convictions, show that the identification of the inverted parallelisms is not enough to reach any definite conclusion either about the theme of the passage or about the convictions that John strives to convey to the readers. Other steps in our structural exegesis will allow us to identify these convictions (steps 2-4) and this theme (step 5). As we draw conclusions from these exegetical steps, we shall be in a position to perceive certain characteristics of the author's faith that are independent of the specific theme and convictions presented in a given discourse unit, namely the characteristics of *the way* of perceiving meaningful human experience presented by the discourse.

2

The Formal Steps of
a Structural Exegesis
(Steps 2, 3, and 4)

METHODOLOGICAL CONSIDERATIONS:
EXPLICIT OPPOSITIONS OF ACTIONS
AS EXPRESSING THE AUTHOR'S FAITH

By identifying a complete discourse unit of the Gospel of John, John 3:1-21, we have identified a passage that should reflect basic characteristics of the entire Gospel as discourse. We have noted that these basic characteristics are nothing else than the author's way of perceiving meaningful human experience that establishes his or her identity as believer; in brief, these are characteristics of his or her faith, or system of convictions. Although this faith is expressed by the theme of a religious discourse unit, it became clear that the study of the inverted parallelisms of a discourse unit is not enough to elucidate these characteristics of the author's faith. For that purpose, other exegetical steps are needed.

For structural exegesis, these other exegetical steps are based upon an understanding of the rules or structures that govern the generation of meaning in and through any discourse. Here we need to take into account the role of certain kinds of oppositions, *oppositions of actions*, in the generation of meaning.[1] One can readily understand why a study of the

---

1. Here, and throughout this book, I avoid referring to the specific features of the semiotic theory that are the basis for the proposed method. For readers interested in refining their theoretical understanding of this method, I briefly mention in notes the aspects of the semiotic theory to which I allude, which can be found explained in Daniel Patte, *The Religious Dimensions of Biblical Texts: Greimas's Structural Semiotics and Biblical Exegesis* (Society of Biblical Liturature, Semeia Studies [Atlanta: Scholars Press, 1990]). Thus, here, I allude to the structures that govern what is known technically as the "surface narrative syntax" and its relations to the "narrative semantics." This is also speaking of the "polemical structure" of narratives and any other discourse. The study of polemical structures (that often involves the use of the actantial model that accounts for the relations among subjects and their opponents) can be the primary focus of a structural exegesis (eventually combined with other methods). Cf., e.g., the use of this structure in John Dominic Crossan, *The Dark Interval: Towards a Theology of Story* (Niles, Ill.: Argus Communications, 1975), 63–87.

oppositions of actions will allow us to identify basic characteristics of the author's faith when one remembers that any faith is grounded in a "system of convictions."[2]

A system of convictions is the perception of human experience that establishes a believer's identity. Convictions, however, are not to be confused with ideas. We control our ideas, in the sense that we produce them (by studying, by reasoning, we develop new ideas). We establish their validity (we only accept as valid ideas that we view as properly demonstrated); we constantly question their validity. By contrast, convictions control us, in the sense that they impose themselves upon us. These are truths that we take to be self-evident, obvious, and thus, that we do not view as needing any demonstration. We also acknowledge that we did not produce them (make them up) by saying about them that everybody knows this, and, in the case of religious convictions, we say that they are revelations (from God). Furthermore, convictions as self-evident truths (i.e., as truths that we do not question) control us in the sense that they have the power to impose certain kinds of behavior upon us. Convictions can drive believers to the most eccentric behavior, such as suffering persecution, giving all their belongings to the poor, or waging ruthless religious wars. Without necessarily engendering such extreme behavior, convictions are constantly shaping, orienting, and motivating believers' lives in all their aspects. As such, convictions establish the believers' identity, that is, a view of themselves, a view of the purpose and meaning of their lives grounded in a view of meaningful human experience in the world and before God.

These remarks[3] are enough to understand that although an author can take the risk to be misunderstood about many issues, he or she cannot afford to be misunderstood about his or her convictions. After all, what is at stake is the author's very identity, that without which nothing makes sense! Thus, in any discourse, the author always makes sure that there will be no possible misinterpretation by readers concerning his or her convictions.

---

2. I introduced the phrase "system of convictions" to designate one of the possible goals of a structural exegesis (cf. Daniel and Aline Patte, *Structural Exegesis: From Theory to Practice* [Philadelphia: Fortress Press, 1978]; Daniel Patte, *Paul's Faith and the Power of the Gospel: A Structural Introduction to the Pauline Letters* [Philadelphia: Fortress Press, 1983], 1–27). This dimension of meaning is one of the primary foci of structural exegeses by scholars using Greimas's theory. Using Greimas's vocabulary, they designate this dimension of meaning as the "semantics" of the text, or its "narrative semantics," or again its "semantic universe," and use the "semiotic square" to represent it. See, e.g. Group of Entrevernes, *Signs and Parables: Semiotics and Gospel Texts*, trans. G. Phillips (Pittsburgh: Pickwick Press, 1978); and most of the studies published since 1976 in the journal *Sémiotique et Bible*.

3. For a more detailed discussion of "convictions" as contrasted with "ideas," see Patte, *Paul's Faith and the Power of the Gospel*, 10–27.

What do we do when we want to avoid being misunderstood? Quite often we are not content to state what we want to communicate; we also stipulate *what we do not mean to say*, so as to remove any ambiguity. In other words, we more or less spontaneously set an *opposition* between what we actually want to say and what we do not want to say. So it is with the convictions that comprise the faith that the author of a religious text wants to convey. Oppositions set in the text are the primary mode of expression of such convictions, because the author cannot take the risk that these convictions might be misunderstood. In sum, in order to identify the convictions conveyed by the text, which are also the theme of a religious discourse unit, we need to find the oppositions that express them.

In any discourse unit, many kinds of oppositions can be perceived. Which among these express the author's convictions? First, we must distinguish between *implicit* oppositions and *explicit* oppositions. For instance, when the text refers to a "mountain" or to a "good deed," readers might perceive an implicit contrast with "plain" or the corresponding "bad deed." But note that in such cases readers are free to set up the opposition themselves. Indeed, while "mountain" can be opposed to "plain," as I suggested, it can also be opposed to "city," "sea," "temple," or to any number of other things that are "not a mountain." Such implicit oppositions cannot be viewed as a direct expression of the author's faith, since the author allows the readers to select the opposition and the connotations through which that aspect of the text needs to be interpreted. *Explicit oppositions, that is, oppositions fully expressed in the text, can be viewed as a direct expression of the author's convictions.*

Yet there are still several kinds of explicit oppositions in any given discourse unit. Among them, which are the most direct expression of the author's convictions? Since convictions have the power to shape the believers' behavior, they lead believers to perform certain actions rather than other actions. When this is remembered, it is clear that the *explicit oppositions of actions* (performed by characters in a discourse) most directly reflect and express the author's convictions.[4] By studying these opposed actions, we can therefore identify characteristics of the system of convictions that, in a religious discourse, the author aims at communicating to the readers, and that the theme of the discourse unit also expresses.

---

4. For a more detailed discussion of the opposition of actions (narrative oppositions) as most directly expressing the author's convictions, see Daniel Patte, *The Gospel According to Matthew: A Structural Commentary on Matthew's Faith* (Philadelphia: Fortress Press, 1987), 5–8.

THE SIX STEPS OF
A STRUCTURAL EXEGESIS
OF A DISCOURSE UNIT

On the basis of the preceding methodological remarks, we can outline a general strategy for identifying basic characteristics of the author's faith (the implied author's faith as inscribed in the text) and for studying their expression in the theme of a religious discourse unit, provisionally identified in the first step of the exegesis. Beyond the first step, there are three formal steps (steps 2, 3, and 4), which, in practice, can be combined in a single stage of the exegesis. We also list here the two additional steps (steps 5 and 6) through which we draw conclusions from the formal study, so as to make clear that we should not expect to reach a complete interpretation of the text as we perform steps 2, 3, and 4 of the exegesis.

Step 1. **Identification of a complete discourse unit** and of its theme (see chap. 1 above).

Step 2. **Identification of the explicit oppositions of actions** in the discourse unit.

Step 3. **Identification of the qualifications through which the opposed subjects** (i.e., the characters that perform the opposed actions) **are contrasted.** This step helps us elucidate a first series of convictions underscored by the oppositions.

Step 4. **Identification of the effects upon the receivers** (i.e., the persons or things affected by the actions) **through which the opposed actions are contrasted.** This step helps us elucidate a second series of convictions underscored by the oppositions.

Step 5. **Drawing conclusions regarding the basic characteristics of the author's faith** expressed in the discourse unit. Through steps 2, 3, and 4, we have identified a series of convictions. The fifth step aims at elucidating the characteristics of the *system* of convictions by showing how these convictions are interrelated in categories posited by the *theme* and its inverted parallelisms (step 1).

Step 6. **Elucidation of the specific features of the discourse unit,** that is, of the ways in which the author expresses his or her system of convictions in an attempt to convey it to specific readers that he or she envisions as being involved in a given historical and cultural situation. At this stage we interpret the metaphors and figurative features of a passage, and discuss the issues concerning the traditions and sources used in the passage and the relationship between author and readers. (These issues are usually considered in the first steps of other exegetical methods.)

STEP 2.
IDENTIFYING EXPLICIT
OPPOSITIONS OF ACTIONS
IN JOHN 3:1-21

The second step of a structural exegesis is quite formal, in the sense that it is difficult to anticipate how the decisions made at this stage will affect the final interpretation of the passage, although these decisions exclude many possible interpretations. Positively, this means that our preunderstandings of the passage are kept in check. Although this step could be combined with the next two steps, it is better to perform it independently so as to preserve its formal character.

Principles for Identifying Oppositions of Actions

This step involves identifying *explicit* oppositions of actions. It is a relatively simple procedure that merely requires a close reading of the text. It is a peculiar reading in the sense that rather than attempting to understand the text (as we usually do), we look exclusively for oppositions of actions. To identify them, we follow three principles.

First Principle. An explicit opposition of actions is expressed in the text by two verbs of doing. The only exception is the case where there is a clear ellipsis (when a verb is not repeated). Verbs of doing (or of action) express that the transformation of a situation takes (has taken, or will take) place,[5] by contrast with verbs of being or having that merely express the state of a situation. Verbs of doing include any verb expressing a physical doing (a doing that transforms a physical situation; e.g., building a house), a cognitive doing (a doing that transforms the knowledge that someone has; e.g., saying something to someone), as well as a reflexive doing (a doing through which a subject transforms his or her own situation; e.g., eating, that is, feeding oneself).[6]

Second Principle. There is an opposition of actions only when, from the point of view of the discourse, one of the actions is positive and the other negative. There is no difficulty in understanding that two positive actions (or two negative actions) are not opposed. Yet in identifying oppositions of actions, we have to keep in mind that the point of view of the discourse and our point of view might be different. For instance, for us, punishments

---

5. Note that in an opposition of actions the verbs of doing can be in different verb tenses or forms (including the passive form).

6. Note that *verbs of emotions* are reflexive verbs of doing. E.g. in John 11:38, "Then Jesus, deeply moved again, came to the tomb," the verb "moved" expresses a transformation of the emotional state of Jesus by Jesus himself. Thus, it could be opposed to the action "not being moved" (if it existed in the text).

by God might be viewed as negative; but for the discourse, in most instances, these are positive actions (e.g., right actions performed by the true God, as appropriate responses to wickedness) which, therefore, are not opposed to blessings from God.

Third Principle. In an opposition of actions, the positive and negative actions must be comparable. This is the case when—

1. Two actions affect in *opposite* manners the *same* (or equivalent) receivers (people or things);[7]

2. Two actions affect in the *same* manner *opposite* receivers (people or things);[8]

3. Two cognitive actions form a *polemical dialogue*, that is, a dialogue where characters confront each other with opposite statements. For instance, in Luke 4:7-8, an opposition of actions is set between "The devil . . . said to him (Jesus) . . ." and "Jesus answered him . . ."

This third principle is also useful in the cases where an action A could potentially be opposed to several actions. If each of these actions is comparable to action A, we have found a *complex opposition*—when a positive action is opposed to several negative actions, or several positive actions are opposed to a negative action. But, in most instances, we find that only one action is actually comparable and thus opposed to action A, despite our feeling that several actions were opposed to it.[9]

By following these principles, the identification of oppositions of actions does not present any difficulty. Actually, the main problem in performing this step of the exegesis is that one has the tendency to identify too many oppositions. Keep in mind that the function of these oppositions

---

7. The formula for such oppositions is: (O– – –>R) vs. (non O– – –>R), where vs. means versus (is opposed to); and O and non–O are opposite Objects communicated to the same (or, equivalent) Receivers (R). An alternate formula is: (O– – –>R) vs. (O– / –>R), that is, the communication or noncommunication of the same Object to the same Receiver. For instance, in Matt. 25:35 and 42, "giving food to the hungry" is opposed to "giving no food (= not giving food) to the hungry," where "the hungry" is the Receiver, and "food" the Object which is or is not communicated. The more general oppositions such as "doing something" vs. "not doing it" (as in Matt. 5:24, 26, "doing" and "not doing" Jesus' teachings) belong to this category, even though the Receivers are not mentioned.

8. The formula for such oppositions is: (O– – – >R) vs. (O– – –>non–R), where R and non–R are opposite Receivers.

9. Actually, if we find that the other actions belong to other oppositions, our feeling that the other actions are "opposed" to action A is indeed correct. A positive action is in direct opposition (contrariety) with the negative action of its own opposition, and also in indirect opposition (contradiction) with the negative actions of the oppositions surrounding it. (The same can be said about the relations of a negative action with positive actions.) To simplify our method, in step 2 we only take into account the direct oppositions, identified with the three above principles. The indirect oppositions are accounted for in steps 3 and 4, as we study the relations among the different oppositions.

is to underscore for the readers certain points that are particularly important for the author. Therefore, we should take into account only those oppositions that can readily be perceived.[10]

The Oppositions of Actions in John 3:1-21

As we read John 3:1-3, we might first wonder whether the first exchange between Nicodemus and Jesus is a polemical dialogue, and thus constitutes a first opposition of (cognitive) actions. Jesus' answer might be somewhat polemical, since he seems to change the topic. Is not Jesus correcting a wrong view implied in Nicodemus's statement? These hesitations should be enough to warn us that it is not clear whether or not the reader (the implied reader envisioned by the author) is expected to perceive this exchange as a polemical dialogue. Thus, we do not record any opposition here.[11]

Yet in Nicodemus's statement "for no one can do these signs that you do" (John 3:2), we note an opposition between *doing these signs* (what Jesus did) and *not doing these signs* ("no one can do these signs" means that other people *do not do* them). Since this opposition is in a statement by Nicodemus, a character who is not trustworthy (as the rest of the text shows, he misunderstands everything!), we will have to be cautious in our interpretation. The opposition might underscore a point of view which is wrong according to the author. Yet we record this opposition.[12]

OPP 3:2 (+) 3:2b Jesus doing signs vs. (−) 3:2a people not doing signs[13]

As we continue our reading, it is clear that Jesus and Nicodemus are engaged in a polemical dialogue. By his questions (3:4), Nicodemus objects to Jesus' saying about "being born anew" (or "from above," 3:3). Yet he simultaneously shows that he misinterprets this saying, as Jesus' next statement (3:5-8) expresses. What is the polemical dialogue opposition? We hesitate. Is 3:4 opposed to 3:3? Or to 3:5-8? Two factors allow us to

---

10. Experience shows that adding oppositions is more misleading than missing some of them. So, when we are in doubt, we do not take into account what could have been an opposition. Numerous examples of diverse kinds of oppositions of actions are proposed in the *Computer Assisted Lessons* entitled "Method # 1 and 2."

11. Even though we shall discover later on that this first exchange is indeed polemical, we do not record it since the reader does not necessarily perceive it.

12. Note that we record the subjects who perform the actions. This is helpful for the next steps of the exegesis.

13. By convention I write the positive action (+) on the left, and the negative action (−) on the right. To facilitate reference to the oppositions (= OPP), I label them with their verse number(s), here as OPP 3:2. Vs. (= versus) separates the opposed actions.

decide. First, as we consider the next and last exchange between Nicodemus and Jesus, it appears that in 3:10 Jesus directly objects to Nicodemus's question in 3:9. In other words, these two sayings form an opposition (see below). This means that Jesus' statement in 3:5-8 is not opposed to the next statement by Nicodemus (3:9). Thus, it is certainly opposed to 3:4. This is confirmed when we note that both 3:4 and 3:5-8 deal with the same topic; both propose interpretations of Jesus' opening statement (3:3), and are thus the most *comparable* cognitive actions.[14]

OPP 3:4-5 (+) 3:5ff Jesus answered vs. (−) 3:4 Nicodemus said

In Jesus' answer, we note an opposition in 3:6 between *being born of the flesh*, a negative action, and *being born of the Spirit*. This positive action is also found in 3:5 as "being born of water and the Spirit." The fact that these verbs are in a passive form (in Greek, a perfect participial passive form in 3:6, and an aorist subjunctive passive form in 3:5) does not prevent them from forming an opposition of actions. But who are the *subjects who perform the actions*? Here, it is fairly easy to identify them. Spirit (and water) and flesh can be viewed as the subjects-agents of the action of "giving birth."

OPP 3:5-6 (+) 3:5, 6b Spirit (and water) giving birth vs. (−) 3:6a flesh giving birth

As we noted, in 3:9-10 we find a polemical dialogue opposition:

OPP 3:9-10 (+) 3:10 Jesus answered him vs. (−) 3:9 Nicodemus said to him

John 3:11-15 begins as a direct response to Nicodemus. Yet we note that, in 3:12, *not believing* what Jesus says is possibly opposed to *believing* ("how can you believe?"). The hesitation comes from the fact that this rhetorical question implies that Nicodemus will not believe. But, in 3:15, the positive action is clearly expressed: "whoever believes in him." Thus, this opposition does exist. We also note that the negative action "not believing what Jesus says" is expressed in another form, "not receiving our testimony," in 3:11. Thus, we note the complex opposition:

OPP 3:11-12, 15 (+) 3:15 Someone believing in Jesus vs. (−) 3:11, 12 Nicodemus not believing Jesus' words, not receiving his testimony

14. Note the vocabulary used by the text for these exchanges. Jesus is the one who "answered him," while Nicodemus is described as taking the initiative (he "said to him"). Once again, this suggests that 3:4 is opposed to 3:5–8 (the polemical response to 3:4).

In 3:13, we note an elliptic opposition of actions in the phrase: "No one has ascended into heaven but he who . . ." Although the text does not repeat the verb clause,[15] it expresses that the Son of man ("he") *ascended into heaven*, while other people did *not ascend into heaven*.[16]

OPP 3:13 (+) 3:13b Jesus ascending into heaven vs. (−) 3:13a People not ascending into heaven

The phrase "should not perish but have eternal life" (3:16) can be viewed as expressing an opposition of actions, although at first one might doubt it. One could object that the second verb, "having," is not formally a verb of doing. Yet here it clearly has an active meaning that can be rendered by "acquiring" or "receiving." A second objection could be that "perishing" is a righteous punishment from God, and thus not negative. From the point of view of the text, however, it is against the will of God that people perish, and thus perishing is negative. The grammatical subject of these verbs, "whoever" (someone), is not the subject that performs the actions; "whoever" is the receiver of the actions (the one affected by them). These verbs have to be treated as if they were in a passive form. The subjects who perform the actions are indefinite. But as is often the case, such passive formulations have "God" (mentioned earlier in the verse) as their subject. In the case of the negative action, the subject is a "false god" (as the next verse makes clear). In recording the opposition we formulate the action in an active form so that the subjects will be clear.

OPP 3:16 (+) 3:16b God giving eternal life vs. (−) 3:16a (False god) making perish

The preceding decision is confirmed by the next opposition that we find in 3:17. It opposes two alternative goals for sending the Son: *condemning the world* (the negative action)[17] and *saving the world*. Condemning, causing people to perish, is not positive for the text, because it is against God's will.

15. The construction of the phrase demands that an ellipsis of ascended be perceived in this phrase, even though the next verbal clause emphasizes the opposite movement. With the repetition of the verb, the verse reads: "No one ascended into heaven but he [ascended into heaven he] who descended from heaven, the Son of man." On the problem raised by the tenses see Rudolf Schnackenburg, *The Gospel according to John* (New York: Seabury Press, 1980), 1:392–94; and Raymond E. Brown, *The Gospel according to John. I–XII*, Anchor Bible (Garden City, N.Y.: Doubleday & Co., 1966), 132.

16. One might hesitate. Is "no one ascended into heaven" negative from the point of view of the text? At first, one might doubt it, since the text wants to underscore that Jesus is the only one who did it. But, when one recognizes that "ascending into heaven" is approximately equivalent to "entering the kingdom" and "having eternal life," it appears that "not ascending into heaven" is indeed negative. This is what people should do, although they could not do so before the coming of the Son of man.

17. As is marked by the negation "not" in the phrase "not to condemn." A negation such as not is used in a discourse either to mark that an action is negative (as is the case here) or to transform a positive action into a negative action (a positive action that is not performed, such as "not believing" in OPP 3:11-12, 15).

OPP 3:17 (+) 3:17b God and the Son saving the world vs. (−) 3:17a False God and the Son condemning the world

In 3:18, we find a similar opposition of actions between *being condemned* and *not being condemned* that can be homologated with the preceding one. In addition, we find again an opposition between *believing* and *not believing*. We take note of it, because the context is different as compared with OPP 3:11-12, 15.

OPP 3:18 (+) 3:18a Someone believing in the Son vs. (−) 3:18b Someone not believing in him

In 3:19, despite an ellipsis, the opposition of actions is clear:

OPP 3:19 (+) 3:19b Someone (loving) light vs. (−) 3:19a Someone loving darkness

Finally, in 3:20-21, the opposition between *doing evil* and *doing what is true* is clear, as is the opposition between *coming to the light* and *not coming to the light*.

OPP 3:20-21a (+) 3:21a Someone doing what is true vs. (−) 3:20a Someone doing evil

OPP 3:20-21b (+) 3:21b Someone coming to the light vs. (−) 3:20b Someone not coming to the light

STEP 3.
THE CONVICTIONS EXPRESSED
BY THE SUBJECTS OF OPPOSED
ACTIONS IN JOHN 3:1-21

Following the identification of the oppositions of actions, we are in a position to identify the convictions that the author underscores in the discourse unit. A first set of convictions is expressed by *the qualifications through which the subjects are opposed* in each opposition of actions.[18]

In the case of a religious discourse, one can say that opposed actions are viewed by the author as having a religious significance. A part of this significance is related to the subjects (characters performing the actions). A glance at the positive subjects of the oppositions of John 3:1-21 is enough to recognize their religious connotations. The subject of four positive actions (OPPs 3:2; 3:4-5; 3:9-10; 3:13) is Jesus who is described as a

---

18. The opposed qualifications of the subjects form *semantic oppositions* (i.e., oppositions of convictions) that are closely associated with the syntactic oppositions (i.e., the oppositions of actions). Another set of convictions is discussed in step 4.

"mediator" between the divine and human beings (cf. 3:13, 16, 17); in three cases (OPPs 3:5-6; 3:16; 3:17), the subject is the divine (God or the Spirit); in five other cases (OPPs 3:11-12, 15; 3:18; 3:19; 3:20-21a; 3:20-21b), the subjects are ideal believers. In other religious texts, religious leaders (such as prophets, priests, rabbis, apostles) also are subjects of positive actions in oppositions.[19] A discourse with such oppositions has the effect of defining the proper views (convictions) that readers should have of these subjects. Thus we can expect that John 3:1-21 expresses convictions about Jesus as mediator, about the divine, and about believers. In this third step of the exegesis, our task is to elucidate these convictions as precisely as possible.

Principles for the Identification of Convictions Expressed by Opposed Subjects

Subjects are often designated by "names," such as Jesus and Nicodemus. A few remarks about names will help us understand how subjects and their qualifications express convictions.[20]

A name expresses the identity of a person, that is, his or her uniqueness. But, at first, a name is an empty label. For instance, a last name picked out at random from the phone book (e.g., Smith) means nothing by itself. By the very fact that it is in a certain context (the phone book), we begin to fill in the label; this name quite probably designates a human being. If a recognizable first name qualifies the last name, then we can deduce that this name designates a woman or a man. Yet, for us, this name is still the equivalent of Jane Doe or John Doe! The address qualifies this name further; it refers to a person living at a specific location. If we recognize this location as a poor or rich neighborhood, then we can imagine a poor or rich person. But the name-label is still quite empty. We are far from knowing the identity of this person. We need more information; we need to know what qualifies this name and makes this person a unique individual. *In sum, we need to know the qualifications that distinguish that person from all other persons.*

This last observation is important for our study. The identity of the person designated by a given name is determined by certain qualifications that set this person apart. Other qualifications or data about that person are not pertinent in the sense that they are not qualifications that set this person apart. This is a common experience. We acknowledge that we do

---

19. Most subjects of positive actions in oppositions belong to one of the four categories just mentioned: Divine, Mediator, Religious Leader, Believer. As we shall see, the category Religious Leader plays a role in John 3:1-21.

20. On proper names, see Louis Marin, *The Semiotics of the Passion Narrative: Topics and Figures*, trans. A. M. Johnson (Pittsburgh: Pickwick Press, 1980), chap. 1.

not truly know a person (the identity of that person), even though we might know a lot of things about him or her.

These remarks about names and the identity of a person apply to the identity of characters in a discourse, whether they are designated by names or not. Certain of the qualifications of a character are not pertinent, in the sense that they do not contribute to establishing what the author sees as the "true identity" of the character (i.e., the author's convictions related to this character). For instance, in John 3:1-21, we can deduce from the name Jesus that he is a man and not a woman; yet, here,[21] this qualification is not pertinent. Jesus' true identity is defined by the qualifications that set him apart from other characters. Thus, the author's convictions about Jesus (the true identity of Jesus according to the discourse unit) are expressed by those qualifications of Jesus that are different from the qualifications of other characters with whom he is compared.

There are two types of comparisons: negative comparisons that we call *contrasts*; positive comparisons that we call *correlations* (or simply, comparisons).[22] First, Jesus is *contrasted* with Nicodemus (OPPs 3:4-5; 3:9-10) and the collective character "people" (OPPs 3:2; 3:12) to whom the text opposes him. The text defines Jesus' identity in a first way by underscoring the qualifications through which he is *unlike* Nicodemus and other people,[23] even though he might share some qualifications with them. Second, Jesus is *correlated* (or compared) with God and ideal believers, that is, with other positive subjects whose identities are also defined by opposition to other subjects. Although Jesus is different from God and ideal believers, he nevertheless shares qualifications with them; in certain ways, he is *like* them.[24] In order to elucidate John's convictions about Jesus, we need to examine both the contrasts and correlations.

One should, of course, be aware of the general rules (or structures) that govern the attribution of qualifications to a character who is also the subject. When we reflect on what a subject must have in order to perform an action, we can recognize that there are two categories of qualifications: certain qualifications contribute to the establishment of the subject's *will*; others give him or her the *ability* to perform this action. A third category

---

21. As we shall see in chap. 4, this qualification is pertinent in John 4:4-42.

22. Semiotics calls the *contrasts* (negative comparisons) either "relations of contradictions" or "relations of contrariety" (a distinction that is not needed for our present purpose), and the *comparisons* (positive comparisons) "relations of implications."

23. In semiotic terminology, one would say that Jesus is in relation of *contradiction* with Nicodemus and "people" (the relation A vs. non A). Secondarily, in some of the cases he is also in relation of *contrariety* with them (the relation A vs. B, where B is the contrary of A, and not merely the negation of A). By discussing the comparisons (relations of implications) we take into account the relations of contrariety, which do not, therefore, need to be discussed separately in this simplified method.

24. In semiotic terminology, one would say that Jesus is in relations of *implication* with God and ideal believers.

of qualifications, the subject's *knowledge*, also needs to be recognized, even though different kinds of knowledge either contribute to the establishment of the will, or give ability. By definition, an action is performed only when a subject has the will, the ability, and the knowledge to perform it.[25]

Qualifications contributing to the establishment of the will. These qualifications include all that convinces the subject to perform the action. Among these qualifications, one finds physical or emotional constraints put on the subject by other people or by other forces: for example, torture, threat of punishment, or flood might be qualifications of the subject insofar as these constraints convince him or her to act in certain ways, even if he or she does not wish to do so. Such qualifications also include commands and orders that the subject readily follows because they are given by someone that he or she recognizes as a good authority figure. And, of course, these qualifications might be simply the recognition by the subject that performing a given action is something good or desirable. In this latter case, the subject is qualified by a certain kind of knowledge—a knowledge of what is good or evil, desirable or not, euphoric (bringing about happiness) or dysphoric (bringing about unhappiness).

Qualifications giving the ability. These include everything the subject needs to use to perform the action.[26] When the action is physical (e.g., building a house), the subject needs physical qualifications, such as strength, tools, lumber, bricks. Note that tools, lumber, and bricks are qualifications that enable the subject to perform the action. Even in the case of physical actions, the subject also needs a cognitive ability; he or she needs to know how to perform the action. In the case of cognitive actions (e.g., teaching), the subject primarily needs knowledge—the professor needs to know what she or he teaches the students. Even in this case, however, physical qualifications (e.g., strength and tools such as books or blackboard) and know-how (e.g., pedagogical skills) are necessary.

When an action has been performed, it means that a subject had the will, ability, and knowledge to perform it. But the discourse does not describe all the corresponding qualifications (which would include such

---

25. Will, ability, and knowledge are subcomponents of the semiotic theory. To be specific, these are discursive expressions of modalities. Certain structural exegeses are focused upon the studies of modalities in texts. See, e.g. Richard Rivar, "Loi ancienne et écriture nouvelle: une analyse sémiotique de Jean 8:2–11," in *De Jésus et des femmes. Lectures sémiotiques* (Montreal: Bellarmin; Paris: Cerf, 1987), 142–45. For a study of modalities in the context of several steps of a structural exegesis, see Group of Entrevernes, *Signs and Parables*, 39–43.

26. Consequently, by contrast with common usage of the term, in this definition, "ability" is not limited to the individual qualifications (strength, skill, know-how) of the subject. Other people, specific circumstances, locations, or times might be part of what enables the subject to act.

things as being alive and breathing!). Even in a highly descriptive discourse, only a limited number of the qualifications of the subject are mentioned, and among these only a few are underscored as particularly significant through contrasts and correlations with the qualifications of other subjects. As readers, we are called to presuppose that the subject has the other qualifications necessary for performing the action. And so we spontaneously fill in the gaps. Yet, as exegetes, we must focus our attention on the qualifications underscored by the contrasts and the correlations. These express the author's convictions concerning the distinctive identity of the subject.[27]

Convictions Expressed by Opposed Subjects in John 3:1-21

In order to elucidate the convictions expressed by opposed subjects, we first examine how each positive subject is contrasted with the corresponding negative subject. Then, as soon as we have studied two oppositions, we examine the correlations that the discourse posits, either among the various positive subjects, or among the various negative subjects. As we proceed, we should remember to record only that which is explicitly expressed by the text. We should expect that in certain cases no convictions will be expressed by opposed subjects; this happens when an opposition of actions is set in order to underscore exclusively convictions related to the effects of the actions (cf. step 4).

OPP 3:2. The positive subject Jesus who does signs is opposed to indefinite people who do not. The category of the qualifications that set Jesus apart is clearly expressed in the phrase "no one *can* do," that is, no one is *able* to do. Jesus has a special ability. What are the qualifications that give him this special ability? The text expresses it in the phrase "unless God is with him" and in the description of Jesus as "a teacher come from God." Jesus is enabled to perform signs because "God is with him" in a special way (since other people do not have this qualification), and/or because he has "come from God," and/or because he is a "teacher" that one can respectfully call Rabbi.

On the basis of this single opposition we cannot reach more definite conclusions. It should also be noted that these qualifications of Jesus have to be interpreted with caution, because they are ascribed to Jesus by Nicodemus. They might include a misunderstanding, or miss the most significant characteristics of Jesus' identity according to John.

---

27. Exegetes using the method of reader criticisms (based on W. Iser's theory) have the opposite goal. They seek to identify the gaps so as to elucidate the competence the author expects the implied readers to have. See, e.g., Richard A. Edwards, *Matthew's Story of Jesus* (Philadelphia: Fortress Press, 1985); and R. Alan Culpepper, *Anatomy of the Fourth Gospel: A Study in Literary Design* (Philadelphia: Fortress Press, 1983).

noted regarding the preceding opposition, the mention of "love" refers to the establishment of the will. In order to be saved, people need to believe in Jesus. But, for this, they need to be willing to believe; that is, they must have a positive evaluation of Jesus (they must love the light). As such, they shall be willing to receive Jesus' teaching (cf. OPP 3:11-12, 15).[38]

OPP 3:20-21b. It is enough to mention that people qualified as loving the light have then the will to "come to the light," while those who love darkness do not.

OPP 3:20-21a. This opposition concerns believers and provides other qualifications for the subjects of the preceding opposition by underscoring the condition for loving the light and believing. In order to be willing to believe, one must "do what is true." If one "does evil," one does not want to come to the light "lest one's deeds should be exposed." "Doing what is true" establishes the will of people to come to the light and thus to believe.

Regarding the opposed subjects of this opposition, note that the positive subject (one who does what is true) is qualified by the mention that his or her "deeds have been wrought in God." Thus, before believing, the future believer is a person who is already "in God." Since there is no corresponding qualification of the negative subject, the text does not specify what "in God" means, although it is somehow associated with "truth" (since doing good is doing what is true). In other words, the text does not specify how the will of people to come to the light is established, since it is not clear what "doing what is true" or "doing deeds wrought in God" means. We could imagine that it means that this person acts "in the presence of God," or "according to God's will,"[39] or again "with the help of God."[40] This point will be somewhat clarified in step 4.

STEP 4.
THE CONVICTIONS EXPRESSED BY
THE EFFECTS OF OPPOSED ACTIONS UPON
RECEIVERS IN JOHN 3:1–21

The results of this step of the structural exegesis are often presented simultaneously with those of step 3, as one studies each opposition. It is,

---

38. The fact that OPP 3:18 and 3:19 emphasize without ambiguity the believer's will confirms our interpretation of OPP 3:11-12, 15. The problem that must be overcome to become a believer is not a lack of ability (as if people were prevented by something or someone to believe, and thus were unable to believe), but a lack of will.

39. In both cases, the relationship with God would establish the would-be believer's will.

40. In this case, God would give that person the ability to do good.

however, a distinct step dealing with other features of the discourse. Rather than considering the opposed subjects and their qualifications, here we consider how the opposed receivers are affected in different ways by the opposed actions.

Principles for the Identification of Convictions Expressed by the Effects of Opposed Actions

Generally speaking, the effect of an action is to transform the qualifications of a receiver. When the receivers are persons (rather than inanimate things), the principles to be used for this step are similar to those of step 3. Since receivers are characters who, in turn, often become subjects of their own actions, in a religious discourse positive receivers often belong to the same categories as the positive subjects: divine, mediator, religious leaders, and believers. Furthermore, their *status* as potential subjects might be affected by the actions of which they are receivers. In other words, as a result of an action, the receiver's will, ability, or knowledge (to do something) might be transformed. Yet the effect of actions might be more general with consequences affecting the very *existence* of the receiver (e.g., killing and giving birth), or the *quality of their life* (e.g., giving them happiness or sorrow, eternal life or condemnation).

The convictions are expressed by the different ways in which receivers are affected by opposed actions. Therefore, as in step 3, in order to elucidate these convictions we study the *contrasts* (between the opposed receivers in each opposition of actions) and the *correlations* (among either positive or negative receivers) posited by the text.

Convictions Expressed by the Effects of Opposed Actions in John 3:1-21

One should remember that the effects of opposed actions are not necessarily emphasized by a discourse. This happens when an opposition of actions merely underscores convictions related to the subjects.[41] This is the case of **OPP 3:2** (doing and not doing signs) in which the receivers are not mentioned.

OPP 3:4-5. In this opposition formed by a polemical dialogue, Nicodemus is the receiver of Jesus' words, and Jesus is the receiver of Nicodemus's words. As is often the case in polemical dialogues,[42] the emphasis is on

---

41. It is because this is often the case that we first study the convictions expressed by opposed subjects.

42. The exception to this rule occurs when the polemical dialogue is formed by commands (to do something) and countercommands, or when as a result of the exchange, the receivers act in new ways, demonstrating that they have been affected by the actions.

the contrast between the subjects and their respective knowledge. The effect upon the receivers is simply to provide them with a knowledge giving them the ability (and, possibly, the will) to continue the dialogue. Thus, in such cases, no new conviction is expressed by the effects of opposed actions.

OPP 3:6. Here at last, the opposed effects of the actions are clearly marked. The effect of the Spirit giving birth to people is that they receive a specific "nature"; they are "spirit." Similarly, the effect of the flesh giving birth to people is that they are "flesh." In other words, the "nature" of someone depends upon the origin of that person. If one's origin is the Spirit, one is spirit; if one's origin is the flesh, one is flesh. The significance of this point appears when we note that there is an additional effect: people have, or do not have, the ability to enter the kingdom of God (cf. 3:5). In sum, for John, in order to be able to enter the kingdom of God, one must have the appropriate nature. One must be "spirit," a nature that is "from above,"[43] "from the Spirit," and thus similar to the kingdom of God,[44] which is spiritual because it is "of God" (who is associated with heaven, and can be said to be above the world, since "God sent the Son into the world," 3:17). When one is flesh, a nature related to the (physical) world, one cannot be associated with the (spiritual) kingdom.[45] In 3:8, we find a further description of people born of the spirit: they are like the "wind" or "spirit" (same word in Greek). Since the wind is qualified by a certain "will" ("the wind blows where it wills"), people born of the Spirit are similarly qualified as having the will to go to certain places that are unknown to other people ("you do not know whence it comes or whither it goes").

OPP 3:9-10. This is a polemical dialogue opposition. The convictions expressed by the effects of opposed actions are the same as those studied in step 3.

OPP 3:13. Since the effect of being associated with heaven is that Jesus has the ability to bear witness and to teach (qualifications of the preceding positive subject), we have accounted for the effects upon receivers in step 3.

---

43. *Anôthen*, the word also translated "anew" in the phrase "born anew."

44. Note that I do not say that "the kingdom of God is itself spiritual *in that it is 'above,' 'in heaven'.*" The evidence of the text does not allow us to say that John envisions a "kingdom in heaven" (Matthew's phrase). The kingdom might be "spiritual" in the same way that believers are "spirit." We have to make sure not to project our preunderstandings on the text. Because of this cautious approach, our exegesis needs to limit itself to the evidence provided by the text to be sure that we do not draw undue conclusions.

45. This conviction is related to that expressed in OPP 3:20-21, where it is emphasized that the subject comes to the light, the Son of God who comes from heaven, only insofar as he or she already acts in God.

OPP 3:11-12, 15; 3:16; and 3:18.   We can treat all these oppositions together because their effects upon receivers are similar. Believers are given "eternal life" (3:15, 16) and are "not condemned" (3:18), by contrast with nonbelievers, who are condemned and perish. The positive comparison with the receivers in OPP 3:6 shows that having eternal life is similar, and even identical, to entering the kingdom of God. Since the ultimate effect of believing and of being born anew is the same, we can say that they are closely associated, yet we cannot say that they are the same things. We also note that believing is defined in two different ways. In 3:11-12, believing amounts to receiving (appropriating) Jesus' testimony or teaching. Yet it is also described as believing in the Son of man (3:14-15), in the only Son of God (3:16), and "in the name of the only Son of God" (3:18). These are two stages of believing. First, believers are people who acknowledge who Jesus is, that is, have the knowledge of the true identity of Jesus (his name) and his uniqueness (*only* Son) as the Son of God or as the Son of man who descended from heaven. Second, and consequently, believers are people who appropriate Jesus' teaching, because they recognize that it is true, authoritative teaching, since it is uttered by the Son of God.

OPP 3:17.   This opposition is similar to the preceding ones with one difference: the receiver of salvation (equivalent to eternal life) is the world. This underscores John's conviction that the Son's coming offers salvation to everyone, and not merely to a select group. Yet, as emphasized in 3:18-19, the essential condition for receiving salvation is an appropriate response, namely, believing. By not believing, one condemns oneself (3:18) because one rejects the only means through which one can receive salvation.

OPP 3:19.   As a result of loving light or of loving darkness, people are willing to come to the light or not.

OPP 3:20-21a.   Although the receivers are not mentioned, the description of these opposed actions is noteworthy. Doing evil, or doing worthless deeds, is opposed to doing what is true. In other words, good deeds are deeds that fulfill the truth. Since Jesus' teaching and testimony are themselves defined as truth (cf. 3:3, 5, 11-13), we conclude that would-be believers (those that come to Jesus) are people who, somehow, already manifest the truth that Jesus also expresses in his teaching. It is in this sense that their deeds are in God.

OPP 3:20-21b.   The effect of coming to the light is that it makes manifest the actual worth of people's deeds. The truth about people is revealed. In other words, encountering Jesus has the effect of making manifest the actual character of what people were doing before the encounter (as with Nathanael in John 1:45-51).

As we try to understand the relationship between these convictions, we note that: (a) doing what is true establishes the will to love the light; (b) loving the light establishes the will to come to the light—Jesus; and (c) coming to the light (Jesus) is itself presented as related to believing (since those who do not come to the light are condemned because they do not believe, 3:18-19). We also note that the effect of coming to Jesus is that the true character of one's deeds is made manifest. When we keep in mind the two stages of believing (acknowledging who Jesus is and appropriating his teaching), it appears that the effect of coming to Jesus demonstrates for would-be believers who Jesus is, namely, the light (since in his presence the nature of one's deeds is made manifest). Coming to the light-Jesus is thus a condition for the first stage of believing; it gives people the ability to recognize that Jesus is indeed the light, and thus the ability to believe in his name, a belief that in turn establishes their will to receive his testimony.[46]

As we conclude the formal steps (steps 2, 3, and 4) of our structural exegesis of John 3:1-21, we note that our study of the oppositions of actions has allowed us to identify a series of convictions (study of the contrasts) and to begin perceiving their interrelations (study of the correlations posited by the text). But we do not have yet a clear understanding of how all these convictions fit together and form a system of convictions. Two additional steps will allow us to complete our structural exegesis by drawing conclusions from this formal analysis.

---

46. This point is also clearly made in 1:45-51, with Nathanael, and in John 4, with the Samaritan woman (see chap. 4).

3

The Concluding Steps of a Structural Exegesis (Steps 5 and 6)

In the preceding steps of the exegesis, we identified a series of convictions by studying the network of relations (contrasts, correlations) posited by John 3:1-21 among the subjects of opposed actions (step 3) and their effects upon receivers (step 4). The fifth step of the exegesis draws conclusions from this study by showing how these convictions form a system by being interrelated according to a *pattern* that characterizes the discourse as a whole (the Gospel of John) as well as the theme of the passage studied. Then, on this basis, the sixth and last step of a structural exegesis elucidates the specific features of the discourse unit (John 3:1-21)—features and issues that other methods study from the outset of their exegesis.

STEP 5.
THE PATTERN OF THE SYSTEM OF
CONVICTIONS EXPRESSED IN JOHN 3:1-21

A system of convictions is best described as interrelating categories of convictions, each category being a set of convictions about a certain domain of human experience or a certain issue.[1] The convictions are

---

1. "System of convictions" designates what Greimas calls the "narrative semantics" or "micro-semantic universe" of a discourse. "Categories of convictions" designates what Greimas calls "semantic isotopies" because they assure the semantic homogeneity of a discourse unit. From the reader's perspective, isotopies are perceived as that which gives coherence to the discourse unit during the reading process. As such the isotopies or categories are directly related to the theme of the discourse unit as discussed below. "Categories" (or "isotopies") are certain of the "codes" that Barthes studies in a text, those codes that organize the entire discourse. Cf. A. J. Greimas and J. Courtés, *Semiotics and Language: An Analytical Dictionary*, trans. L. Crist, D. Patte, et al. (Bloomington: Indiana University Press, 1982; French, 1978), 163–65; 277; and Roland Barthes, *S/Z: An Essay*, trans. Richard Miller (New York: Hill & Wang, 1974).

organized in each category according to a certain pattern.[2] This pattern is the most characteristic aspect of an author's faith—and thus of the discourse as a whole—because all the categories of a system of convictions follow the same kind of pattern.[3] It represents the specific *way* of perceiving meaningful human experience that characterizes a given faith. This can be demonstrated by considering a general example.

In many religious discourses, convictions about God and about humankind form a *pattern* that expresses the relationship between God and humankind. Similarly, convictions about family members (e.g., parents, children) often form a pattern that expresses the relationship among family members. As suggested by the metaphorical use of names of family members to express the relationship of God (e.g., Father in heaven) with human beings (children of God), the same pattern of relationship is found in both domains of human experience; the relationship between God and human beings is similar to (follows the same pattern as) the relationship among family members, or vice versa. Then, in our example, when we study a discourse unit that is exclusively concerned about, for instance, family relationships, by identifying this pattern we also identify the pattern that characterizes the relationship between God and humankind,[4] even if this discourse unit does not mention it! We identify a pattern that is characteristic of the system of convictions of the author, and thus of the discourse as a whole.

In order to elucidate the pattern formed by the convictions of a discourse unit, we need to identify (1) the *categories* (corresponding to issues or dimensions of human experience) that the discourse itself uses to regroup convictions, and (2) *how convictions are organized* in each category—a hierarchical organization that forms a pattern. This pattern should be the same in all the categories of convictions of the discourse

2. This "pattern" is what Greimas calls the "axiology" of a narrative semantics; this axiology is posited in the "fundamental semantics." See Greimas and Courtés, *Semiotics and Language*, 21, 275–76.

3. It is this pattern that many structural exegeses based on Greimas's semiotic theory seek to represent in the abstract form of a semiotic square of semantic features that displays the "axiology" of the discourse. For diverse uses of the semiotic square as a representation of the axiology of text, see the works by Genest, Calloud, Panier, Gueuret, Group of Entrevernes, as well as Daniel Patte and Aline Patte, *Structural Exegesis: From Theory to Practice* (Philadelphia: Fortress Press, 1978); and Daniel Patte, *The Religious Dimensions of Biblical Texts: Greimas's Structural Semiotics and Biblical Exegesis* (Society of Biblical Literature, Semeia Studies [Atlanta: Scholars Press, 1990]).(See Annotated Select Bibliography). In the practice of structural exegesis, it is better to avoid having recourse to such abstract formulations that, for many, hide the signification of the text rather than reveal it. I propose a way of elucidating this pattern by using concrete terms of the text.

4. As well as the relationship of convictions about other domains of human experience (e.g., relationship of convictions about members of the church, or about the church and the world, or about various parts of the cosmos).

unit and of the discourse as a whole, since its characteristics are characteristics of the author's faith—of the author's way of perceiving meaningful human experience. When a discourse unit involves several categories of convictions (as is the case in John 3:1-21), one can verify that the pattern is the same by comparing the respective organizations of the convictions in these categories. Yet, since certain discourse units have a single category of convictions, we need principles that will allow us to identify such patterns in a single category.

Principles for the Identification of Categories of Convictions

Since our first task is to identify the categories that the discourse itself uses to regroup convictions, we must avoid imposing upon the discourse categories that it does not use. We need to beware of our preunderstandings that define our own categories; the categories that are meaningful for us might be quite different from those of the discourse. For instance, for us, the "family" is usually a category (a domain of human experience) that we primarily envision in terms of kinship relations. Yet in other cultures, a "family" might primarily be envisioned in terms of economic relations. Thus, we might not recognize that economic relations (e.g., between master and servants) mentioned by a discourse belong to the category "family" as much as the relations between parents and children (which, in this example, would also be viewed as economic relations—parents providing what children need). We have to beware of our preunderstandings about any category, but especially about religious categories.

How should we proceed? First, we need to remember that a religious discourse aims at communicating convictions to the readers. These are the convictions that the *theme* of the unit and its inverted parallelisms express in general terms, and that the oppositions express more precisely. Actually, the theme limits itself to presenting the main categories of convictions of that unit.[5] By considering the inverted parallelisms (step 1) in light of the convictions discovered through the study of the oppositions (steps 2, 3, and 4), we can identify the categories of convictions that the discourse posits, rather than projecting our own categories upon the text. Other categories of convictions might also be found in the same unit, especially if it is long; these are subcategories expressed by the themes of sub-units. They are to be interpreted in terms of the categories posited by the main theme.

---

5. Technically, the *theme* of a discourse or a discourse unit is a dimension of the "discursive semantics" of the text. It is posited by the implied author (enunciator) as an expression of his or her system of convictions (narrative semantics) for the implied reader (enunciatee). The expression of this theme in figures (its figurativization) will be studied in step 6.

In practice, we soon discover that these categories of convictions are organized around convictions regarding the subjects and receivers of opposed actions. Since in religious discourses these subjects and receivers often include the divine, a mediator, religious leaders, believers, and opposed characters (antidivine, antimediator, bad religious leaders, nonbelievers), categories of convictions can often be designated as categories of convictions about these subjects and receivers. Remember, however, that each category interrelates convictions. In this light, we can formulate the kinds of relations that each of these frequently encountered categories might involve. Being aware of the full range of potential relations is important to avoid reading into the text our own categories of convictions (focused on certain of these relations).

Category of convictions about the divine. This category should be viewed as one that expresses the *relationship* of God with everything else or, more specifically, the relationship of a certain view of (a conviction about) God with certain views of (convictions about) everything else. It is helpful to be aware of the kinds of relations that are potentially involved in such a category.

- Relations of God with the *world* in general and/or the cosmos;
- Relations of God with *people*, that might be expressed by the effects of divine interventions upon various people (individual persons, communities, or nations);
- Relations of God with *places* (where God is present or intervenes);
- Relations of God with *times* (times when God has intervened, intervenes, or will intervene; sacred times).[6]

Category of convictions about the mediator. This category should be viewed in a similar way as expressing the relationship of the mediator with everything else (the world, people, places, times, and, of course, God).

Category of convictions about religious leaders. This category involves similar kinds of relations. It usually emphasizes the relations of leaders

---

6. The focus on relationships with people, places, and times is not haphazard. It is derived from a part of the universal structure that governs discoursivization: "discoursive syntax" that includes the processes of actorialization, spatialization, temporalization. More precisely, by considering these three processes together, we identify the "thematic roles" (the types of roles played by the main characters in space and time). When one considers the thematic roles of the characters involved as subjects or receivers of opposed actions, one identifies the concrete representations of the system of convictions in a text (its syntactical representation for the implied reader or enunciatee). Structural exegeses can be devoted primarily to the study of one or the other of these processes. The studies in Adèle Chené, et al., *De Jésus et des femmes*, are primarily devoted to the elucidation of the actorialization of women in their relations to Jesus in Gospel texts. Similarly, the study by Elizabeth Struthers Malbon, *Narrative Space and Mythic Meaning in Mark* (San Francisco: Harper & Row, 1986), is entirely devoted to the study of spatialization in the Gospel according to Mark.

with people who are led—the relations of *religious authority*—as well as the relations through which persons are established as religious leaders (relations concerning the origin of their authority). Relations with places and times, of course, should not be neglected.

Category of convictions about believers. This category involves all the relations through which people become believers (among which are relations with God, the mediator, religious leaders), as well as the relations that characterize people's life as believers (e.g., relations with other believers, relations within the community of believers, individual or communal relations with nonbelievers and the rest of society; the relations that should characterize the fulfillment of their vocation). Relations with places and times might also be significant.

When dealing with these and other categories of convictions (e.g., those concerning the antidivine, antimediator, bad religious leaders, nonbelievers), we identify which of these relations are expressed,[7] and how each of these relations is specified in the discourse unit.

Principles for the Identification of the Pattern of Convictions in Each Category

As we identify a category of convictions, we discover in it a series of relations. For instance, in the category concerning believers, we might find that a given discourse emphasizes relations of the believers to the message of a mediator, of the believers to other people expressed in the form of good deeds, of the believers to the kingdom that they hope to enter, and many other relations. The questions are: How are the convictions expressed by these relations organized? According to which pattern? In brief, they are hierarchically organized according to the *hierarchies of values* posited by the text.[8]

Relations to things, persons, and situations (relations that can be expressed as actions) are valued either as more or less good or as more or less evil (or bad). For instance, the ultimate good might be having eternal life (e.g., the situation of one who is in the kingdom of God, with God). Believing (e.g., a believer's positive response to a message) as well as doing good deeds might be other "goods" that are needed to enter the kingdom. These are "lesser goods" that can be organized according to

---

7. Of course, one should be alert for all the relations expressed by the text, which will often include other relations not mentioned above.

8. Here, I refer to another aspect of the structures that govern "fundamental semantics" (Greimas's terminology). When considering earlier the "relations" (among discrete entities of human experience) identified in the delimitation of categories of convictions, we considered the "veridictory" categories of the discourse. Now, by studying the "hierarchies of values," we consider the "thymic" categories of the discourse. See Patte, *The Religious Dimensions of Biblical Texts* (chaps. 3 and 4).

their relative position vis-à-vis the ultimate good. For instance, if, according to a given discourse, one must believe in order to be in a position to do good deeds, then what is valued as good is in the following hierarchical relationship (with a progression toward the ultimate good):

1. believing,
2. good deeds,
3. entering the kingdom.[9]

Relations to things, people, and situations that are valued as more or less evil are in a parallel hierarchical relationship.[10] In our example:

1. not believing,
2. evil deeds,
3. perishing in hell.

Of course, in most discourse units, the lists of positive and negative values are much longer, and the corresponding hierarchical relationships are more complex. But this example is enough to understand that a system of convictions is, in part, a system of values; it is the way in which one perceives values in the various aspects of human experience. Such a hierarchical pattern of values is found in each category of convictions (that concerns exclusively positive values, since they are convictions about the divine, the mediator, religious leaders, or believers). Yet, in most cases, the category of convictions about believers represents the pattern more clearly, because the discourse units provide a more complete hierarchy of convictions about believers. As we shall further discuss in the "Conclusion," the comparison of different faith-patterns is best done by comparing the hierarchies of convictions about believers found in two texts.

---

9. The organization of the hierarchy of convictions follows the unfolding of the (usually hypothetical) story of an ideal believer (or, in other cases, of another category of characters). This is so even though we are speaking here of convictions (and not of the plot of a story), because of the relationship between "narrative syntax" (including narrative plots) and "narrative semantics" (system of convictions). See Patte, *The Religious Dimensions of Biblical Texts*, chaps. 2, 3. As will be clear in our examples, this narrative-like hierarchy usually does not follow the plot of the discourse unit, for the simple reason that it amounts to reconstructing the plot of a hypothetical story of a *type of characters* (rather than the story of an actual character). The elucidation of such hierarchies can be the primary focus of a structural exegesis. This is what Petersen does in his study of Philemon and other Pauline texts, even though he uses a different technical vocabulary (in part borrowed from sociology of knowledge theories). He reconstructs what he calls the "referential sequence" (that corresponds to the ordering of the "hierarchy of convictions") out of the "poetic sequence" (that I called "plot of the discourse unit") to gain access to the "symbolic universe" of the text ("system of convictions" or "semantic universe"). See Norman Petersen, *Rediscovering Paul: Philemon and the Sociology of Paul's Narrative World* (Philadelphia: Fortress Press, 1985), 43–88, passim.

10. The fact that the two hierarchies are parallel provides us with an important interpretive tool. If it is not clear what is the hierarchical relationship among the various goods, one can deduce it from the hierarchy of evils. Yet, note that in a system of convictions the hierarchy of positive values (goods, blessings) is primary. In other words, in most instances, it is the hierarchy of goods which is to be used to clarify the hierarchy of evils. The negative values are often presented by characters with a "wrong" point of view, and thus also with a "wrong" pattern-hierarchical organization—"wrong" according to the discourse.

This is so because the hierarchies of convictions of the other categories necessarily intersect with the hierarchy of convictions about believers.[11] Both the divine and the mediator intervenes on behalf of believers or would-be believers, as religious leaders, who are themselves believers, also do. But, since our purpose in this chapter is to demonstrate that all the categories of convictions have the same hierarchical pattern, we shall treat all the categories of convictions equally and shall limit ourselves to a study of the hierarchy of (positive) convictions in each of the categories.

In sum, in each category of convictions, we consider not only the relations of characters (e.g., believers) with the world, persons, places, times (usually already identified by the study of the correlations in steps 3 and 4), but also the hierarchical relationship of these relations according to their positive and negative values. The hierarchy of convictions of each category which is established in this way is a concrete representation[12] of the *pattern* that characterizes the system of convictions of the entire discourse—a concrete representation of the *way* of perceiving meaningful human experience that characterizes the author's faith. Of course, a given category of convictions, or even all the categories of a given discourse unit, do not present all the implied author's convictions. Consequently, the hierarchies will always be incomplete. But, the pattern that they represent is recognizable.

The Pattern of Convictions in John 3:1-21

Identification of the Primary Categories of Convictions. In step 1, we noted with inverted parallelisms that the theme of John 3:1-21 posits two primary categories; we also noted a secondary category:

— Convictions about Jesus (as mediator): the Son of God sent as the light of the world (3:18-21) rather than merely as a teacher come from God (3:1-3).

---

11. And with the corresponding hierarchy of evils. Since the hierarchy of convictions about believers includes many blessings brought about by the interventions of the divine, the mediator, and religious leaders who overcome certain "evils," this hierarchy can be called the "hierarchy of blessings," as one contrasts it with the "hierarchy of evils." Here, because of space limitations, we do not present a systematic study of the hierarchy of evils. Yet, we do so in some of the Computer Assisted Lessons, and thus we use this terminology as a shorthand.

12. As mentioned above, in this simplified method, we do not propose to seek to elucidate the abstract semantic pattern ("axiology") that undergirds such concrete representations. This next step of the analysis is quite important in that it allows identification of the specificity of a system of convictions (i.e., its most fundamental characteristics). Yet, in my experience, this next step is more confusing than helpful, because it demands to deal with minute semantic features ("semes"). One can much more directly appreciate the specificity of a given pattern of convictions by comparing and contrasting it with the patterns of convictions found in other discourses (see below, chap. 5 and the conclusion).

— Convictions about believers and, more specifically, about people's responses to Jesus: coming to the light (3:19-21) rather than coming at night, in darkness (3:2).

— A secondary category of convictions about religious leaders is found in John 3:1-12. It is posited by inverted parallelisms between 3:1-2 and 3:10-12, concerning Nicodemus and Jesus as teachers.

Therefore, we need to deal with three categories. Since they give coherence to the discourse unit, they should be found throughout the passage. This is the case of the convictions about Jesus, as we have shown (steps 3 and 4). But the convictions about believers and about religious leaders seem to be located in two different parts of the unit. The convictions that are unambiguously about believers are found in 3:12-21, while in 3:1-12 (3:12 functions as a hinge between the two sections, a frequent phenomenon) the convictions about believers also seem to apply to religious leaders. The references to those who are "born anew/from above" seem to designate believers, because they refer to an undetermined number of people ("every one"), rather than to a few leaders, and because being born anew/from above is a condition for entering the kingdom. But in 3:7, "Do not marvel that I said to you [singular], 'You [plural] must be born anew,' " this phrase is applied to a group that would include Nicodemus, a religious leader (a ruler of the Jews), and 3:10-11 clearly speaks about religious leaders (teachers). Nevertheless, the ambiguity remains; "every one" designates believers more readily than a limited number of religious leaders. These remarks are enough to suggest that we should consider the convictions about believers in 3:12-21 separately from the convictions about believers or religious leaders in 3:1-12 before considering their relationship.

By focusing on these categories, we leave aside some of the convictions expressed by two oppositions: convictions about the Spirit (OPP 3:5-6) and about God (OPP 3:16). These are obviously related to convictions about believers/religious leaders and Jesus, respectively. We shall have no difficulty accounting for them.

The Pattern of the Convictions about Jesus.   Let us list the convictions about Jesus that we have identified in steps 3 and 4. Here, we are primarily concerned with the positive convictions (that have been underscored by being contrasted with negative convictions). We also leave aside Nicodemus's (wrong) understanding of Jesus (3:2). We have noted the following convictions:[13]

---

13. In the formulation of these convictions, we note the specific ways in which Jesus is related to God, people, and places. Here, time does not appear to play any role.

— Jesus has true knowledge that gives him the ability to be a true teacher for people such as Nicodemus (OPP 3:4-5).

— Jesus is able to be a true teacher of whoever receives his words in that he speaks of what he knows, and bears witness to what he has seen (OPP 3:9-10).

— Jesus, and Jesus alone, has descended from heaven and ascended there (OPP 3:13).

— Jesus, the only Son, is sent by God (characterized by his love for the world and his will to save the world); Jesus brings salvation to the world (OPPs 3:16, 17).

— Jesus as the light makes manifest the true character of people's deeds (OPP 3:20-21b).

As we seek to understand how these convictions are hierarchically interrelated, we see that all of them concern Jesus' mission and his qualifications to carry out this mission. Thus, the ultimate good is Jesus bringing salvation (i.e., eternal life) to the world. When this is recognized, the hierarchical relationship appears:

1. Jesus is in heaven (3:11) and has firsthand knowledge of heavenly things (3:16-17);
2. Jesus is sent into the world, descends from heaven (3:16-17);
3. Jesus is thus able to bear witness not only about earthly things but also about heavenly things (3:11-12); Jesus is light of the world (3:20-21) and true teacher (3:4-5);
4. Jesus ascended to heaven (3:13) because he must be lifted up (3:14);
5. Jesus gives eternal life to people.

In this hierarchy, the first four stages are clear. It is because Jesus is in heaven that he can be sent into the world and can descend from heaven; his coming into the world is a condition for bearing witness; it is after bearing witness that he ascends to heaven by being lifted up. But it is not clear in the discourse unit why he must be lifted up and ascend to heaven in order to give eternal life to people. We suspect that a number of convictions belonging to this stage of the hierarchy of John's system of convictions are not underscored in John 3:1-21.[14] Yet the main pattern is clear.

On the basis of our theoretical considerations, we can conclude that, if we have correctly established it, this hierarchy is a concrete representation (in terms of certain convictions about Jesus, more specifically, about

---

14. So far, we have taken into account only the convictions that the discourse unit underscores by its oppositions. These are the convictions that the discourse unit strives to convey to the implied reader. Other convictions might be expressed in other ways by the unit (see step 6).

his mission) of a faith-pattern that should organize in a similar way convictions about other categories of human experience. In the case of John 3:1-21, we can verify that it is the case and refine our perception of this pattern, since this unit presents at least one other category of convictions (about believers), and possibly a third one (about religious leaders). So that our verification might be as impartial as possible, we proceed to identify the hierarchy(ies) of the other category(ies) without taking into account our findings regarding the convictions about Jesus.

The Pattern of Convictions about Believers in John 3:12-21.   In steps 3 and 4, we have identified the following convictions about believers:
— Believers are willing to receive Jesus' testimony; they have a secondhand knowledge; they are also people who believe "in Jesus" the Son of man (OPP 3:[11], 12, 15).
— Believers are to receive eternal life (OPP 3:16, cf. also 3:15) and not be condemned; for this, they need to believe "in the name of the only Son of God" (OPP 3:18).
— Believers love the light, and thus have a positive evaluation of Jesus (OPP 3:19).
— Would-be believers "do what is true" and their deeds are performed "in God"; they are associated with "truth" and "God" in some way (OPP 3:20-21a).
— Believers are willing to come to the light (OPP 3:20-21b).

The hierarchical relations of these convictions appear as soon as we note that in order to believe in Jesus, the light, people need to come to the light, and that for this purpose they need to do what is true.

1. Would-be believers are in God and have (some) truth (3:21);
2. They do "what is true" (3:21);
3. They are thus willing to come to the light (that reveals the true character of their deeds, 3:19-21);
4. They believe in Jesus, in the name of the only Son (3:18; they recognize that he truly is the "light," because he reveals the true character of their deeds, 3:19-21);
5. They believe (receive) Jesus' testimony (since they acknowledge him as the only Son, the light, they can trust his testimony, 3:11b-12, 18); They have a secondhand knowledge;
6. Ultimately, they receive eternal life (3:15, 16, i.e., they are saved, 3:17).

Once again, we suspect that there might be several stages of the hierarchy of convictions missing between the last two stages. We simply wonder whether nothing else happens to believers after they receive Jesus' testimony as a condition for receiving eternal life or entering the kingdom.

The Pattern of Convictions about Believers or Religious Leaders in John 3:1-12. We first list the convictions that we have identified in steps 3 and 4 of the exegesis, including the convictions regarding what, according to Jesus' words, an ideal Nicodemus should have done.

— Having true knowledge by taking into account the activity of the Spirit and religious matters (something that Jesus does, but that Nicodemus should also do); being born anew/from above of the Spirit; being born anew as that which enables people to see and enter the kingdom of God (OPP 3:4-5);

— Being spirit; having the will to come from, and go to, places unknown to other people (OPP 3:6);

— Having firsthand knowledge (seeing) and bearing witness to what one has seen; having received Jesus' testimony (secondhand knowledge); being able to see (OPP 3:9-10).

The hierarchical order of these convictions is not clear. First, how is being born anew related to bearing witness and to seeing? Since 3:10-12 is a response to Nicodemus's question regarding being born of the Spirit, the general phrase "we bear witness to what we have seen," among other things, refers to bearing witness to the action of the Spirit which causes people to be born anew/from above. In order to bear witness about being born anew, one first needs to see. That is, one needs firsthand knowledge (see OPP 3:9-10, step 3) of what is involved in being born of the Spirit. Then who can give a testimony regarding being born of the Spirit? We are asking: To whom, in addition to Jesus, does "we" refer in 3:11 ("*We* bear witness to what *we* have seen, but you did not receive *our* testimony")? A strong possibility is that "we" also refers to those who are born of the Spirit.[15] They are those who are in the best position to have firsthand knowledge of what is involved in being born of the Spirit! Thus there is a hierarchical progression from being born anew, seeing, and bearing witness.

We have noted (see OPP 3:9-10, step 3) that receiving the testimony of Jesus and others (receiving secondhand knowledge) is also necessary for being able to see. Thus, receiving the testimony precedes seeing, as does being born anew. The question is, What is the hierarchical relationship between receiving the testimony and being born anew? Since receiving Jesus' testimony is the same thing as believing what Jesus says (3:12), the question becomes, Does one need to believe Jesus' testimony before being born anew (of the Spirit) or vice versa? Many interpretations seem to imply that being born of the Spirit is the initial step for becoming

---

15. For other possibilities, see Rudolf Schnackenburg, *The Gospel according to John* (New York: Seabury Press, 1980) 1:375–76 and note.

a believer,[16] without explicitly raising the question of the relationship of believing Jesus' testimony and being born anew. But, since the direct condition for seeing is being born of the Spirit, we have to conclude that believing Jesus' testimony, that is, receiving secondhand knowledge, is an indirect condition for seeing, and thus precedes being born anew in the hierarchy. This proposal that believing (in Jesus' testimony) is a condition for being born anew is confirmed by 3:5. In this verse, Jesus explains that being "born anew" means being "born of *water* and the Spirit" (3:5). Since water refers to baptism, and since people who go to be baptized are people who have received Jesus' testimony (see the next discourse unit, 3:22—4:3), we conclude that believing Jesus' testimony is a condition for being born anew/from above. Thus, we find the following hierarchical order:

1. Believing Jesus' testimony (3:12) as the condition for being born of the Spirit;
2. Being born of the Spirit (and thus being spirit, having the will to come from, and go to, places unknown to other people, 3:5-8);
3. Then one has firsthand knowledge and is in a position to bear witness to the role of the Spirit in people being born anew (to bear witness to "earthly things"), and thus to be a true "teacher of Israel" (3:10-12);
4. One can then enter the kingdom of God (the ultimate good).

Of course, this interpretation hangs on the possibility that "we" refers to those born of the Spirit. This hierarchy must, therefore, be justified by pointing to other pieces of evidence, namely, by comparing this proposed hierarchical pattern with the pattern formed by the convictions about Jesus (see below), as well as with the pattern found in other discourse units (see the study of John 4 in chap. 4 below). A first confirmation of the validity of this interpretation is found in the fact that John 3:1-12 is a sub-unit because it is the direct discourse between Jesus and Nicodemus, a teacher of Israel. Since the "we" in 3:11 designates ideal teachers, that is, *what Nicodemus should be*, and since according to 3:7, *Nicodemus should ideally be born anew*, it follows that ideal teachers ("we") are those who are born anew. Furthermore, we now understand why we found it difficult to decide whether the convictions of 3:1-12 belong to the category of believers or religious leaders. It now appears that every believer needs to be born anew so as to be in a position to carry out his or her vocation,

---

16. This is the interpretation suggested by Raymond E. Brown, *The Gospel according to John I–XII*, Anchor Bible (Garden City, N.Y.: Doubleday & Co., 1966), 140. Brown follows the ancient patristic interpretation found in the *Shepherd of Hermas*, Justin, Irenaeus, and Augustine (cf. I. de la Potterie, "Naître de l'eau et naître de l'Esprit," *Sciences Ecclésiastiques*, 14 [1962]: 351–74). See also Schnackenburg, *John*, 368.

which is to bear witness to what he or she has seen. Every believer is to be a true teacher of Israel. The two preceding hierarchies actually form a single hierarchy, which can be read beginning with the series of convictions found in 3:12-21 and continuing with the series found in 3:1-12.

1. Would-be believers are in God and have (some) truth (3:21);
2. They do "what is true" (3:21);
3. They are willing to come to the light (that reveals the true character of their deeds, 3:19-21);
4. They believe in Jesus, in the name of the only Son (3:18; they recognize that he truly is the "light," because he reveals the true character of their deeds, 3:19-21);
5. They believe (receive) Jesus' testimony (since they acknowledge him as the only Son, the light, they can trust his testimony, 3:11b-12, 18); they have a secondhand knowledge; this is the condition for being born of water and of the Spirit;
6. They are born of the Spirit (and thus are spirit, and have the will to come from, and go to, places unknown to other people, 3:5-8);
7. They then have firsthand knowledge and are in a position to bear witness to the role of the Spirit in people being born anew (to bear witness to "earthly things"), and thus to be a true "teacher of Israel" (3:10-12);
8. They can enter the kingdom of God (3:5) and have eternal life (3:15-16), the ultimate good.

The Faith-Pattern Represented by the Hierarchies of the Two Categories. As we compare the hierarchies of the convictions about Jesus and about believers, we could note how these categories intersect. Thus, one could not come to the light and believe (stages 3, 4, and 5 of the category about believers) if Jesus had not been sent into the world and did not bear witness (stages 2 and 3 of the category about Jesus). Yet this is not the point of our comparison. Here, we do not seek to integrate these two categories into a single one.[17] Rather, we want to verify whether they are concrete representations (in terms of two different domains of human experience) of the same pattern—as our theoretical considerations led us to expect.

As we examine the hierarchies of convictions about Jesus and believers, it does not take long to recognize that the same pattern organizes them. This is apparent when we consider the convictions concerning the believers as they carry out their vocation (the believers who are born anew).

_____

17. As one does to establish an overall "hierarchy of blessings" (see below, Conclusion).

— As Jesus is from heaven (3:13) and thus "from above," so believers are born "from above" (3:3-7).

— As Jesus is sent by God (3:17), so believers are born of the Spirit (3:3-7); both "Jesus in the world" and "believers as born anew" have a divine origin (they are from God or from the Spirit).

— As Jesus is the "only Son of God" (3:16-18), bearing the name of the One who sent him, so believers are "spirit" (3:6) sharing the nature of the One who caused them to be born from above. Thus, we conclude that the phrase "Son of God" also expresses that Jesus shares the nature of the One who sent him.[18]

— As Jesus bears witness to what he has seen both on earth and in heaven (3:11-12), so believers bear witness to what they have seen (on earth) by taking into account the role of the Spirit ("we" in 3:11).

— Furthermore, Jesus ascended into heaven because he *must* be lifted up (3:14, i.e., according to the will of God); thus, as he carries out his vocation according to the will of God who sent him, he comes from, and goes to, a place unknown to people (since he is the only one who has been in heaven). Similarly, believers born of the Spirit are like the wind-Spirit that "blows where it wills" (their will is similar to the will of the Spirit), and they come from and go to places unknown to others (cf. 3:8) as they carry out their vocation.

— Finally, as Jesus ascended to heaven (3:13), so believers born of the Spirit will enter the kingdom of God (3:5).

Thus, although the concrete representations of the pattern in terms of convictions about Jesus and about believers are quite different, it is nevertheless clear that these two categories are organized along the same pattern. As, according to our general example, divine-human relationships and family relationships are often conceived along the same pattern and thus are "alike," so the vocation of Jesus and the vocation of the believers follow the same pattern and are "alike." This is not to say that the vocation of believers is the same as that of Jesus. The discourse emphasizes that Jesus' mission is unique, because he is the only one who is in a position of bearing witness to heavenly things, and thus to bring eternal life to the world. But, by bearing witness to earthly things, believers contribute to this mission, although, in John 3:1-21, it is not clear in which way they do so.[19] More importantly, the similarity in pattern means that believers

18. As is, of course, expressed in other passages from the Gospel according to John (e.g., 1:1).

19. The similarity in pattern between the convictions about the mission of Jesus and about the vocation of the believers who are born of the Spirit is a decisive confirmation that "we" (in 3:11) must be interpreted as referring to Jesus and those who are born of the Spirit.

are like-Jesus. This observation confirms that, in John's system of convictions, Jesus as mediator and believers are indeed categories of convictions; they are two of the dimensions of human experience that are perceived in terms of the basic pattern used by John to make sense of each of these domains. We can then suspect that the rest of the pattern of convictions concerning believers (i.e., the rest of the hierarchy concerning their becoming believers) also applies to Jesus. We can expect that—

— As people are willing to come to the light (and thus become believers) because, earlier, they were already doing what is true in God, so Jesus was willing to carry out his ministry (being sent into the world to save the world) because, earlier, he was already doing what is true in God.

This is, of course, what is expressed in John 1:1-3 that underscores (with an opposition in 1:3) that the preexisting Son of God, the Word, participated in the divine activity of creation.

The establishment of the hierarchies of convictions in the categories about Jesus and about believers and their comparison allow us to perceive clearly the pattern that characterizes John's faith. We might want to attempt to formulate it more abstractly, to clarify the specificity of the characteristics of John's faith. We refrain from doing so (although such a step of exegesis can indeed be performed), because a more meaningful way of apprehending the specificity of a faith is to compare the concrete representations of its pattern (the hierarchies of convictions) with similar concrete representations of the patterns of other kinds of faith. This is what we shall propose below, in Chapter 5 and Conclusion.

STEP 6.
DISCERNING THE SPECIFIC FEATURES
OF THE DISCOURSE UNIT

Through the preceding steps of the structural exegesis, we have identified a basic pattern of convictions that characterizes the Gospel of John as a whole. We do not claim to have identified all its convictions and all the aspects of this pattern; the study of other passages would help us refine our understanding of this pattern. This is why we present exegetical exercises on another passage of the Gospel of John (see chap. 4 below). Yet if we have not made too many errors in our exegesis, the pattern we have identified should also be found in this other discourse unit, whether it deals with the same categories of convictions (about Jesus and believers) or with other categories. Before examining this other passage, we need to complete our study of John 3:1-21 by elucidating its specific features.

Principles for Studying the Specific Features of a Discourse Unit

In order to understand how to proceed, we must remember that the goal of a religious discourse is to communicate a faith to readers. The Gospel of John makes it explicit in 20:31: "These [signs] are written that you may believe that Jesus is the Christ, the Son of God, and that believing you may have life in his name." We must, therefore, take into account the communication process through which an author (the implied author) strives to communicate his or her faith to certain readers (the implied reader). It is a matter of convincing readers to accept the author's faith as their own. This is a process through which what one wants to communicate is put in the form of a discourse addressed to certain people so as to convince them.[20] This process, including the interaction of an author (enunciator) with readers (enunciatee), shapes the specific features of each discourse unit.

What is involved in communicating a faith? As we noted in chapter 2, the faith that one wants to communicate by a religious discourse is, ultimately, a *way of perceiving meaningful human experience* that establishes people's identity as believers. We can now understand that this way of perceiving is nothing else than the pattern used to make sense of the different dimensions (categories) of human experience; it is the pattern through which convictions are organized in each of the categories of a system of convictions. In other words, a faith is communicated to someone when that person adopts this pattern as a way of perceiving the entirety of his or her experience. The communication of a faith is, therefore, not merely a matter of communicating a knowledge of this pattern (as a structural exegetical discourse does by describing this pattern), but rather a matter of communicating *how one perceives with the help of this pattern*.

How is such a faith-pattern communicated? This can only be done by proposing specific examples of the way in which specific domains of human experience are perceived by following this pattern. Thus a religious discourse as a whole, as well as each discourse unit, presents the faith-pattern as it is actualized in certain categories of convictions. Theoretically,

---

20. Technically, this is the process of "discoursivization" governed by "discursive structures." They include "discursive syntactic structures" (the processes of actorialization, temporalization, and spatialization) and "discursive semantic structures" (the processes of thematization, and figurativization), themselves governed by the overall process of enunciation (the relations between enunciator and enunciatee). On these structures and their application for the study of religious discourses, see Patte, *The Religious Dimensions of Biblical Texts*, chaps. 4 and 5. This dimension of meaning is the primary focus of structural exegeses based upon Bakhtin's theory of discoursivization. See Robert Polzin, *Moses and the Deuteronomist: A Literary Study of the Deuteronomic History* (New York: Seabury Press, 1980). Since in steps 1 and 5 we have dealt with aspects of discursive syntax and thematization, we are here primarily concerned with the "figurativization."

it does not matter which categories are selected for this purpose, since each one embodies the faith-pattern. Certain categories of convictions, however, are selected to be the theme of a discourse (or discourse unit), because they are viewed by the author as the most effective ways of communicating his or her faith to specific readers.

We draw two conclusions from these observations. First, what a religious discourse or discourse unit seems to be about—its theme—is actually the means to communicate something else, a faith-pattern. Of course, the discourse aims at communicating certain convictions; in John 3:1-21, convictions about Jesus and about believers. But these convictions should not be viewed as the ultimate goal of the communication process. A religious discourse (by contrast with "informational discourses," such as scientific discourses) does not aim at communicating a static message (doctrines about Jesus and about believers), but at communicating a way of perceiving, a faith-pattern. Second, since the communication of the convictions that form the theme of a discourse (unit) is the means that an author uses to communicate a faith-pattern to specific readers, we conclude that the author chooses a given theme because he or she sees it as the most appropriate in a specific discoursive situation. [21]

Certain categories of convictions are chosen to be the theme of a discourse (unit) as the author strives to make the discourse convincing for the readers. *For this, the author must be perceived as trustworthy by the readers.* [22] Selecting a certain theme rather than another is a part of the process through which the author establishes his or her trustworthiness. Out of the many categories of convictions of his or her system of convictions, an author chooses a few categories that will hopefully establish him or her as a trustworthy figure in the eyes of the envisioned readers. In this way, the author adopts a "selective identity," an identity as "implied author" or enunciator. Thus, in John 3:1-21 and in the rest of the Gospel, the author chooses to present himself as one who has convictions about Jesus and about believers; he presents himself as a believer in Jesus, rather than, for instance, as a citizen from a particular region, or as a member of a family. Conversely, these categories are chosen as a theme

21. These observations have many implications for hermeneutics that are not unlike those proposed by Bultmann regarding hermeneutics as demythologization. Indeed, in new discoursive situations the most appropriate way to communicate the faith-pattern expressed by the text of John might be discourses that propose the actualization of this faith-pattern in categories of convictions other than those selected by John for the readership he had in mind.

22. As Greimas puts it, a "fiduciary" contract needs to be established between enunciator (implied author) and enunciatee (implied reader). The establishment of the enunciator's trustworthiness is especially important in the case of religious discourses, since they involve the communication of a faith-pattern that will be new for readers, demanding that they give up at least a part of what constitutes their identity.

for the discourse because the author expects it to be meaningful and important for the readers—otherwise, this theme would not establish the author's trustworthiness for these readers. Thus we can conclude that John envisions readers who are themselves believers in Jesus. Such envisioned readers are called the "implied reader" or *enunciatee*, so as to make clear that they might or might not correspond to the actual readers that the author has in mind.

In sum, the convictions that we have identified through steps 1-5 of our structural exegesis of John 3:1-21 are the part of John's system of convictions that John chooses to underscore in his attempt to convince certain readers to adopt his faith-pattern. This means that John expects his readers to be interested in issues related to believing in Jesus. They are people who already believe in Jesus, but, from his point of view, they do not have the true faith-pattern (or, at least, they risk losing it). If they already had this faith-pattern, then it would be pointless to attempt to convince them to adopt it.

Such a religious discourse demands much from the readers; accepting the discourse and its message involves, for them, giving up at least a part of what establishes their identity (their old faith-pattern). Consequently, they must be convinced to acknowledge the validity of the partial system of convictions expressed by the discourse. *This is achieved by expressing these convictions in terms of the readers' old views.* In other words, so that the readers will accept his or her point of view, the enunciator strives to express his or her own convictions in terms of some of the readers' views that the enunciator can also accept. Then, the readers (if they correspond to the enunciatee) are faced with the dilemma of having to reject a part of their own convictions if they refuse to accept the discourse and its new point of view (that requires them to abandon another part of their system of convictions). If the trustworthiness of the enunciator is well established, then they might be inclined to accept the discourse.

The specific features of each discourse unit result from the enunciator's effort to express his or her convictions in terms of the enunciatee's point of view, so that the latter might accept the faith-pattern expressed by the convictions underscored by the discourse. This process gives rise to "figures of speech" of many kinds. For instance, metaphors as a way of speaking of something in terms of something else are figures through which the enunciator expresses his or her views in terms of the enunciatee's views. The effect, as has often been noted, is not merely to communicate a new specific view, but indeed to open up the possibility of a new way of envisioning human experience;[23] a new faith-pattern is being communicated. Other discursive stratagems (e.g., use of literary genres, of direct

23. See Paul Ricoeur, *The Rule of Metaphor*, trans. Robert Czerny (Toronto; Buffalo: University of Toronto Press, 1977).

and indirect forms of speech, reference to traditions and to commonly accepted truths) have similar functions; they establish the trustworthiness of the enunciator, and/or aim at leading the enunciatee to identify himself or herself with the discourse.

In short, the specific features of a discourse unit come from the discoursive process through which the enunciator attempts to convince the enunciatee to adopt a new way of perceiving human experience—the enunciator's faith-pattern. Studying these specific features in John 3:1-21 will allow us to understand more concretely the role of the discoursive process in the meaning-production of a discourse. In so doing, we perceive the profile of the readers (enunciatee) that John envisioned, and we recognize the strategy that he used in his attempt to convince them.

The Specific Features of John 3:1-21

We have noted that the choice of a theme about Jesus and believers shows that the enunciator John presents himself as a believer in Jesus, and that he expects his enunciatees-readers to be believers themselves, although with an inappropriate kind of faith. In order to communicate his faith-pattern to them, John expresses his own convictions about Jesus and believers in terms of views he anticipates that his readers have. Since we have already identified the enunciator's convictions, by reading the text again we can understand how each specific feature of John 3:1-21 expresses these convictions in terms of the enunciatee's views. Let us consider the text verse by verse, taking note of the way in which John seeks to convince the readers to adopt his convictions. For this purpose, we seek to reconstruct how John's implied readers would have read the text for the first time.

John 3:1. The description of Nicodemus as "a man of the Pharisees" and as "a ruler of the Jews" leads the readers to view Nicodemus as a religious leader. But the figure of Nicodemus as a Jewish religious leader is quite ambivalent. The fact that he is designated as a Pharisee and ruler of the Jews suggests that he might be a bad religious leader, because the Jews are presented as misunderstanding Jesus' deeds and words in 2:18-21; readers are expected to have as a part of their old views the knowledge of the preceding discourse unit.[24] At the same time, however, this Jewish

---

24. The "old knowledge" that a discourse unit presupposes the readers have, might be a view that the readers had before the discourse, or a view that previous discourse units had already established. In order to recognize this "old knowledge" that the *implied reader* is supposed to have, we consider the figurative features of the text. Those features that are not part of the enunciator's convictions (i.e., the convictions underscored by the "contrasts" and "comparisons" of the subjects and receivers of the oppositions of actions; see steps 2–5) should be viewed as referring to the "old knowledge" of the implied reader.

leader is designated by a proper name, Nicodemus. This conveys that he might be a special case, and that he might not be as bad as the other Jews are.

John 3:2. For the readers, the ambivalence of the figure of Nicodemus is partially removed by his description as "coming to Jesus." Coming to Jesus (as the disciples did in 1:35-51) is a good thing to do. He might be a Jewish leader in the process of taking the first steps toward becoming a disciple. That he is coming to Jesus by night might be taken as a negative factor. Of course, by the end of the discourse unit, it becomes clear that Nicodemus's way of coming to Jesus by night shows that he is one of those who "love darkness" and do not want to come to the light (3:19-20); he is one of those who do evil and hate the light (3:20). Thus he does not recognize that Jesus is the "light [that] has come into the world" (3:19). But, in 3:2, the readers do not yet know this ("backreading" is not yet possible).[25] They might associate Nicodemus's coming by night with the negative connotations attached to darkness in 1:4. But this does not demand that the readers view Nicodemus negatively, since 1:4 expresses that "the darkness has not overcome [the light]," and "the light shines in the darkness." One can thus interpret this description of Nicodemus's coming as referring to the original situation of any would-be believer. Narratively, one can also interpret this description as referring to an effort of Nicodemus to hide his coming to Jesus from antagonistic Jews (and thus as an effort to separate himself from them), if it could be shown that the implied readers are expected to have anti-Jewish views.[26] We have to conclude that at this point Nicodemus is viewed positively by the readers, since he comes to Jesus, even if this takes place by night.

Thus, the text expects that the readers will at first view Nicodemus's statement about Jesus positively. His characterization of Jesus as "a teacher come from God," because of the "signs" he performed, appears to them to be a valid statement about Jesus. It is only through a "backreading" that this statement is recognized as wrong. In other words, John expects the implied readers to acknowledge readily the validity of this view of Jesus. Since the introduction of a discourse unit is expressed according to the point of view of the readers so that they will readily acknowledge the validity of the discourse (see step 1), we can conclude that John uses here what he expects his readers to believe. In sum, John expects his readers to be people who believe in Jesus because of the "signs" that he

---

25. As one proceeds to read the full text, one is led to reinterpret what precedes in light of the new perspective provided by the new parts of the text one has read. This is what I mean by "backreading."

26. One would need to study the earlier references to the Jews (1:19-28; 2:13-22).

performed; he has authority as a teacher (he is "from God" and "God is with him") because he is a miracle worker. For such readers, in order to believe in Jesus' words, one must first believe in him as a miracle worker. A part of John's goal is to cause his readers to abandon this wrong view of Jesus.

We can begin to recognize John's discoursive strategy. At the beginning of the discourse unit, where John has to show himself as a trustworthy enunciator, he cannot antagonize his readers by straightforwardly rejecting one of their basic convictions. John expects that his readers hold the conviction that in order to believe in Jesus' words one must first believe in him as a miracle worker, and anticipates that they will not easily abandon this conviction. Consequently, he attributes this view to an ambivalent character, making sure that, at first, his readers will view him as a positive character. Indeed, their positive evaluation of Nicodemus (based on his designation by a proper name and the mention of his coming to Jesus) is reinforced by his expression of what they take to be a correct view of Jesus. In this way they are enticed to identify themselves with Nicodemus. For the moment, the fact that the discourse associates Nicodemus with negative characters (Jews, Pharisees) and describes him as coming by night is occulted. By subsequently showing that Nicodemus totally misunderstands Jesus and is, after all, a bad religious leader, the discourse will lead the readers to renounce their identification with Nicodemus. Then they will also be led to abandon their own view of Jesus that they had associated with Nicodemus.

John 3:3. Even though the text reads, "Jesus answered him," at first it seems that Jesus' words introduce a new topic instead of being a response to Nicodemus; while Nicodemus speaks about the way to identify a true teacher "come from God" (3:2), Jesus speaks about a condition for seeing the kingdom. Consequently, the readers do not perceive the first exchange as a polemical dialogue, continue to hold their positive view of Nicodemus, and interpret Jesus' words as referring to conditions for becoming true believers that will enter the kingdom.[27]

Yet following our study of the text's entire set of oppositions and its pattern of convictions, we can recognize (as the readers will also do through a backreading) that 3:2-3 actually form a polemical exchange. By speaking

---

27. Of course, for the readers, Jesus' answer is legitimate. For instance, they might presuppose that Jesus addresses an issue that is behind Nicodemus's statement. Commentators often propose interpretations that show that they are trapped in the role that John expects the readers to play! Schnackenburg (*John*, 366) and Barnabas Lindars (*The Gospel of John*, New Century Bible Commentary [Grand Rapids: Wm. B. Eerdmans; London: Marshall, Morgan & Scott, 1972], 150) fall into this trap, but Brown (*John I–XII*, 138) avoids it.

of being born *anôthen* (anew or from above) and of seeing the kingdom, Jesus speaks about conditions for being a true religious leader. The role of a religious leader is to "bear witness to what [one has] seen" (3:11), which includes "earthly things" and "heavenly things" (3:12). Thus, people who see the kingdom are the only ones who can bear witness to the kingdom; and in order to see the kingdom, one needs to be born from above (*anôthen*). The condition for being a true religious leader is not to perform signs (a physical reality), but rather to be born from above (a spiritual reality) and see the kingdom (a spiritual reality).

Thinking that Jesus has changed the topic and that his words are not a polemical answer, the readers can continue to identify with Nicodemus. Indeed, they do the same thing as Nicodemus will do in his response: they misinterpret Jesus' words for the same reasons. For them, true religious leadership is based on the observation of physical manifestations (signs as miracles), and thus Jesus has changed the topic when speaking about "spiritual" realities.

John 3:4. The readers readily perceive Nicodemus's interpretation of Jesus' statement as wrong, especially when reading Jesus' polemical response (3:5-8). How can one have so crude an understanding of Jesus' words? Of course, Jesus does not refer to entering a second time into one's mother's womb! He is speaking about a spiritual reality. Thus, the readers disassociate themselves from Nicodemus regarding this interpretation. Yet they still do not have any reason to reject Nicodemus's earlier statement (3:2). They can view this dialogue as confirming their earlier interpretation; Nicodemus's blatant misunderstanding shows how much he needs Jesus' teaching! He was indeed in great need to come to Jesus.

John 3:5-6. Accepting this response of Jesus, the readers are led to adopt central convictions of John regarding Jesus as a true teacher who reveals spiritual realities. One feature of the text, however, creates a tension and shows that John expresses his convictions in terms of the readers' views: "unless one is born of water and the Spirit." The mention of water alongside the Spirit is sometimes treated as resulting from an ecclesiastical redaction.[28] Recent commentators[29] reject this interpretation because there is no textual evidence to support it; yet note that the theme of water as allusion to baptism is at most secondary, since the passage emphasizes the contrast between Spirit and flesh. For a structural exegesis, such tensions signal that the author expresses his or her convictions in terms

---

28. This is the interpretation of Rudolf Bultmann, *Das Evangelium des Johannes* (Göttingen: Vanderhoeck und Ruprecht, 1941, 1962), 98. Similar interpretations are proposed by others: K. Lake, Wellhausen, Lohse, Braun, Léon-Dufour, Van den Bussche, Feuillet, Leal, De la Potterie, as Brown (*John I–XII,* 142) points out.

29. Schnackenburg, *John,* 369; Brown, *John I–XII,* 142–43; Lindars, *John,* 152.

of the readers' views. There is a tension because two different perspectives are brought together to make a single point.

From our study of the oppositions, we know that John aims at conveying the convictions that to be a true religious leader one needs to become "spirit" as a result of being "born of the Spirit." Thus, the phrase "born of water" expresses what is meant by born *anôthen* in terms of the readers' views. As recognized by all commentators, this is a reference to baptism. We conclude that John expects his readers to view baptism as an essential rite for believers.[30] By associating "born of the Spirit" with "born of water," John makes it possible for the readers to relate Jesus' words to their own view of the Christian experience, a view that emphasizes the importance of sacraments such as baptism. The abstract views proposed by John are given concreteness; they refer to their concrete experience as believers.[31] Yet, simultaneously, this association of "born of water" with "born of the Spirit" has the effect of transforming the readers' view of baptism. It should not merely be viewed as a baptism of water; it is also and primarily a baptism of Spirit.[32] Indeed, the overall effect of 3:5-8 is to show that what is important in baptism is not so much its physical reality (water), but its spiritual reality; people become spirit.[33]

John 3:7. The injunction, "Do not marvel," shows that John anticipates that this last point will be perceived as surprising by the readers who have identified themselves with the "you" (singular) to whom Jesus addresses his words in 3:5. While the readers do not identify themselves with the actual Nicodemus (3:4), they identify themselves with the ideal Nicodemus presented in Jesus' words. That this identification of the readers with the ideal Nicodemus is indeed what John anticipates is betrayed by the fact that he introduces a plural "you" in the phrase, "You must be born *anôthen*" (3:7). From the readers' point of view, it is surprising that baptism would involve the transformation of a person into a spiritual being.[34]

---

30. At this point, the readers do not yet interpret these verses as referring to religious leadership.

31. This is what Greimas would call the generation of a "referential illusion."

32. This point has already been made in 1:30-33 where John's baptism with water is contrasted with Jesus' baptism with the Holy Spirit. Baptism will be the theme of the next discourse unit, 3:22—4:3.

33. Our structural exegesis helps resolve the debate about sacramentalism in John (see Brown, *John I–XII*, 141–44; Schnackenburg, *John*, 369–70). On the basis of John 3:1-21, we can suspect that the references to sacraments in John are a discursive stratagem. According to John's own convictions, sacraments are not essential for the Christian experience; a spiritual experience is. But, for the sake of his readers, he readily accepts the value of sacraments, provided that one recognizes the spiritual reality they involve.

34. Consequently, it is unlikely that John alludes to biblical and postbiblical traditions (e.g., Ezek. 36:25-26; Isa. 44:3; Jubilees 1:23-25; 1QS 4:19-21) regarding the eschatological outpouring of the Spirit bringing about a new creation of the believers (cf. Brown, *John I–XII*, 140; Schnackenburg, *John*, 370–71), with the expectation that these traditions would be recognized by the readers. Yet the Johannine convictions had their origin in such traditions, as becomes clear in the following verses, which show John reinterpreting eschatological motifs.

John 3:8. Metaphors are figures of speech particularly appropriate to communicate a surprising view. John creates a simile by playing on the two meanings of the word *pneuma* which, in Greek, means both "spirit" and "wind."[35] The wind is described as something that one can hear, although one does not know "whence it comes or whither it goes." But this image becomes strained when the wind is presented as having a will ("The wind blows where it wills"). This makes clear, as we see at the end of the verse, that this description of the wind is simultaneously a description of "every one who is born of the Spirit."

John 3:9-11. The following exchange makes it clear that all the discussion about "being born *anôthen*" is about conditions for religious leadership. Most of the features of these verses are direct expressions of John's convictions. The expected effect of 3:9-11 for the readers is that they will make a backreading of the preceding verses. In so doing, they are led to reject Nicodemus as a bad religious leader (a bad teacher of Israel). For them, remaining identified with him becomes more and more difficult. Consequently, the view that Nicodemus expressed in 3:2 becomes more and more questionable, even though it happens to be their own view of believing in Jesus. John entices the readers to replace their view of believing in Jesus (believing in him because he performs signs) by a view of believing in Jesus because of his unique testimony. John does so by his use of plural personal pronouns in 3:11. Readers will not identify themselves with the "you" who do not receive Jesus' testimony, but will identify themselves with the "we" who, together with Jesus, bear witness, that is, with people who are trustworthy witnesses because they are born of the Spirit. In the process, readers have accepted the definition of a trustworthy witness as a person who "bear[s] witness to what [he or she has] seen."

John 3:12-13. As in the preceding verses, most of the features of 3:12-13 are direct expressions of John's convictions, continuing the strategy of these preceding verses. Since Jesus is the only one who has been in heaven, he is the only one who can be a trustworthy witness of heavenly things. Consequently, readers are led to adopt the view that one should believe in Jesus as a trustworthy witness, a teacher from God, not primarily because "God is with him" as the signs he performs show (3:2), but rather because he is "from above." At this point, the readers' original convictions (expressed in 3:2) are in the process of being displaced.

Other discoursive features are the uses of the title "Son of man" and the verb tenses. The past tenses show that John writes with his readers

35. As the corresponding Hebrew term, *rûah*, also does.

in mind; from the narrative perspective, the ascension is future, and not past, as it is for the readers: for them, Jesus is now in heaven.[36] Similarly, the title Son of man is not required as an expression of John's convictions that are totally focused on the heavenly origin of Jesus. It is a figure that John uses because he expects his readers to recognize it. Taking into account 3:17-18, we can say that John expects his readers to use the title Son of man as a designation of Jesus as the eschatological judge. Following traditions of apocalyptic origins (Daniel, Enoch, Baruch), the readers view Jesus as the Son of man because he ascended to heaven. John affirms this view of his readers together with his own conviction regarding Jesus' heavenly origin, so as to integrate his point with their own beliefs.

John 3:14. This entire verse is discursive, since it does not express John's convictions directly by means of oppositions. This is further shown by the allusion to the story of Moses lifting the serpent in the wilderness that calls upon the readers' knowledge of Scripture (Num. 21:9ff), and by the allusion to the cross ("so must the Son of man be lifted up") as salvific. As it is presented here, John's special way of speaking about the cross as Jesus being "lifted up" (cf. 8:28; 12:32-34) is discursive; it is a figurative way of speaking which makes sense for the readers that he envisions. In other words, John expects his readers to understand the cross as salvific in terms of Numbers 21. Yet by associating being lifted up (on the cross) with the ascension to heaven of the Son of man, John already challenges their view that Jesus' relation to heaven has to be viewed in terms of judgment (see our comments on 3:17-18). For John, the ascension has to be viewed as salvific, in the same way as the cross is.

John 3:15-16. All the features of these verses are the direct expression of John's convictions. The title "the only Son of God" is now used, with the presupposition that the readers will also accept this title as valid. These verses further reinforce the view of Jesus as "from above" (and thus, sent by God), and that his coming from above is not aimed at condemning the world.

John 3:17-18. Most of the features of these verses are the direct expression of John's convictions (they are involved in oppositions). Yet the negative points ("not to condemn the world" and "is condemned already") are related to the figure of Jesus as Son of man. Thus we recognize that John challenges his readers' eschatological views. The Son is not to be viewed as a judge (the readers' understanding of the Son of man). This

---

36. With many commentators, I view the variant reading "the Son of man who is in heaven" to be the original text, precisely because it does not fit the points (convictions) that John strives to express.

does not mean that there is no judgment. But it is not a future, eschatological judgment, as they believe. Rather, this judgment is already taking place for those who do not "believe in the name of the only Son of God."

John 3:19-21. The concluding verses turn completely upside down the views that John anticipates his readers to have (according to the above analysis). First, they believe that the heavenly Jesus is the Son of man as the eschatological judge. But people who perceive Jesus from such a negative perspective (as someone to be feared) are precisely those who are condemned. They are those who hate the light and love darkness. Those who truly believe are those who view the heavenly Jesus from a positive perspective, namely, as the light, that is, as the only Son of the God who loves the world, as the one who brings from heaven what people need in order to be saved. Thus, contrary to what the readers thought, it is not by what Jesus did in the physical world (signs and the cross) that one is saved. Rather, people are saved by the reality from above (*anôthen*; heavenly things) that Jesus reveals as manifested in the world (earthly things) in the transformation of believers into spirit operated by the Spirit. Finally, one cannot say that the trustworthiness of Jesus as a teacher from God is grounded in signs that show that God is with him. Indeed, one can say that God is with would-be believers that do what is true (3:21), although such people are hardly trustworthy witnesses, since they have not yet come to Jesus.[37] The trustworthiness of Jesus comes from his being from above, the Son of God who was with God in heaven and ascended to heaven.

In this reading we have not dealt with all the details of the text. But by dealing with the main figurative features of the text, we have elucidated a few characteristics of the implied readers envisioned by John and the discoursive strategy that John uses in his attempt to convince the implied readers to adopt his pattern of convictions, his way of perceiving human experience, his faith.

---

37. Since the description of doing what is true as "wrought in God" is a discoursive feature aimed at correcting the wrong view that readers have of God's relation to Jesus, it becomes clear that this description of would-be believers is figurative (done in terms of the readers' old views as expressed in 3:2), and thus not necessarily a direct expression of John's convictions. In other words, it is not necessary that one of John's convictions is that would-be believers are already righteous people whose deeds are already "wrought in God."

PART TWO

EXERCISES IN STRUCTURAL EXEGESIS: JOHN 4:4-42 AND LUKE 10:21-42

Introduction to Exercises in Part Two

In Part One, a single passage, John 3:1-21, was studied in detail to serve as an example for the interpretation of other religious texts. This presentation showed that a complete structural exegesis is best conceived as involving six successive steps. Each of these steps examines a specific dimension of the meaning of the text: its "theme" marked by inverted parallelisms (step 1); its polemical character expressed by oppositions of actions (step 2); the convictions of the enunciator expressed in two different ways (steps 3 and 4); the faith-pattern of the enunciator's system of convictions (step 5); and the specific features of the passage generated in the effort to convince the enunciatee to accept the enunciator's faith-pattern (step 6). The order proposed for the performance of these steps is dictated by the need to study specific dimensions as a preparation for the study of other dimensions.

This exegetical procedure makes clear that, for structural exegesis, the "meaning of a text" is multidimensional. What a reader commonly perceives as *the* meaning of a text—a one-dimensional meaning—is actually the overall effect produced by the interactions of several dimensions of meaning. This observation is important for understanding the diversity of structural exegetical procedures.

In most instances, we are not interested in all the dimensions of meaning of a text. We do not study a text for learning everything that can be learned about it and from it, but because we expect to find something that concerns us—answers to specific questions that, consciously or subconsciously, we bring to the text. From the perspective of structural exegesis, this means that we are primarily interested by one or another of its dimensions of meaning, or even by a single aspect of one of these dimensions. Consequently, in most cases, we want a structural exegesis that deals as directly as possible with this specific (aspect of a) dimension of meaning by bracketing out discussion of the dimensions of meaning which are not relevant for the question at hand. This is what most of the structural exegeses mentioned in notes and in the bibliography do. This procedure is quite legitimate, provided that we avoid confusing this dimension of meaning with other dimensions. To avoid such confusion, it is best to perform, or at least to sketch, the analysis of the other steps of the structural exegesis, even though they do not deal with the dimension of meaning that is the focus of our study.

What are the specific exegetical goals that a structural exegesis can have? What specific issues will structural exegesis allow us to elucidate in a text? Such questions are misleading, in the sense that they presuppose that structural exegesis would merely allow us to address a limited number of exegetical issues. As historical-critical methods have the potential of dealing with any possible issues raised by a text,[1] so structural exegesis has the potential of developing procedures for elucidating any issue with which one might be concerned about a text, since it can theoretically deal with all the dimensions of meaning of a text. The structural and the historical-critical approaches are two parallel and complementary ways of elucidating the meaningfulness of a text.[2] But, because of its specific strategy and procedures, each approach is better equipped to deal with certain issues.

For example, structural exegesis *can* address issues concerning the sources and traditions used by an author in redacting a text, or concerning the historical situation of the community envisioned as the readers of the text. But it can only do so at the very end of a complete structural exegesis, by drawing cumulative conclusions from the six steps of the exegesis of all the discourse units of that text.[3] Historical approaches, however, deal with these issues much more directly, at the very beginning of their investigation. Consequently, in the case of such issues, historical-critical methods should have the primary role by being used first; structural exegesis can then be used to complement historical studies by providing additional criteria for addressing unresolved questions and debated points.

Conversely, historical-critical exegesis can address issues concerning the discursive strategy used by an author and the characteristics of the

---

1. Of course, both historical-critical and structural exegeses might conclude that a given text does not provide the evidence necessary to address a question we raised concerning a specific issue.

2. For a detailed explanation of this point, see Patte, *The Religious Dimensions of Biblical Texts: Greimas's Structural Semiotics and Biblical Exegesis* (Society of Biblical Literature, Semeia Studies [Atlanta: Scholars Press, 1990]), Introduction, chaps. 1, 3.

3. As I suggested by a few comments in step 6 of our study of John 3:1-21 (chap. 3 above).

religious teaching of a text, including the theology and the faith (system of convictions) of the author. But it can only do so at the end of a complete historical-critical exegesis, by drawing cumulative conclusions from studies of the specific features of all the passages of the text and from studies of the issues concerning sources, traditions, redaction, and historical setting. Structural exegesis, however, deals with these issues much more directly. Important characteristics of the discoursive strategy of an author can be elucidated in step 6 of the structural exegesis of a single discourse unit.[4] More significantly, steps 3, 4, and 5 of the structural exegesis of a single discourse unit allow us to reach significant conclusions regarding an essential aspect of the religious teaching of a text; namely, regarding the faith-pattern of the system of convictions that the author aims at communicating to the readers. Consequently, in the case of such issues, structural exegesis should have the primary role by being used first; historical exegesis can then be used to complement structural exegesis by providing additional criteria for addressing unresolved questions and debated points.

Since structural exegesis is uniquely equipped to elucidate basic characteristics of the religious teaching of a text, I have proposed to make this elucidation the primary goal of my structural exegeses. The elucidation of the author's system of convictions and faith-pattern addresses many of the questions that we bring to the biblical texts when reading and studying them. With such a goal, the structural exegesis can be limited to steps 1 through 5, and thus can reach significant results relatively quickly. As the examples provided in the following chapters show, the performance of these steps is not as complex as may first appear. Yet one needs some practice. This is what the structural exegeses of John 4:4-42 and Luke 10:21-42 provide.[5] They are designed as exercises for using steps 1-5. The first exercise (chap. 4) is devoted to another text from John in order to show that the same faith-pattern is found in several discourse units of the same text. In this way, our affirmation that the study of a single discourse unit of a text elucidates basic characteristics (the faith-pattern) of the religious teaching of an entire text will be demonstrated. The second

---

4. Or by studying an entire text with the more focused method (that corresponds to step 6 by itself) proposed by Robert Polzin in *Moses and the Deuteronomist: A Literary Study of the Deuteronomic History* (New York: Seabury Press, 1980).

5. In addition, the Computer Assisted Lessons offer the possibility of performing a series of such structural exegeses on one's own, in constant dialogue with experienced structural exegetes, instead of merely reading structural exegeses. These lessons include studies of texts from Mark, Luke, John, the Gospel of Thomas, an early Rabbinic Midrash (the *Mekilta*), and the Dead Sea Scrolls (the *Rule of the Community*).

exercise (chap. 5) is devoted to Luke 10:21-42, a text quite different from the other texts studied.[6]

The significance of the results of such a structural exegesis becomes clear as soon as one has studied discourse units of two different religious texts. Because one can compare their respective faith-patterns (Conclusion), one fully appreciates what characterizes the religious teaching of each. When the results of such studies of several New Testament texts are compared, the differences among the several types of early Christian faith that they present readily appear.

6. Many other examples of the application of steps 1–5 can be found in Daniel Patte, *The Gospel According to Matthew: A Structural Commentary on Matthew's Faith* (Philadelphia: Fortress Press, 1987) (although the steps are not labeled, because in this commentary the focus is on the results of the exegesis). In Daniel Patte, *Paul's Faith and the Power of the Gospel: A Structural Introduction to the Pauline Letters* (Philadelphia: Fortress Press, 1983), the same method is used upon Pauline texts, but the focus is on the application of one step or another upon each given text.

4

First Exercise in
Structural Exegesis:
John 4:4-42

We have already established that John 4:4-42 is a complete discourse unit (step 1; see chap. 1). Since this is an exercise, I simply give
the results of the identification of the oppositions of actions (step 2)[1] in
the process of performing steps 3 and 4. The results of these latter steps
are presented together, as is often done in practice. This procedure is
further required in the case of this passage, because most of the oppositions
are in the form of a chainlike succession of polemical dialogues; the receivers (studied in step 4) of a first exchange become the subjects (studied
in step 3) of the following exchange. Yet it is essential to perform these
two steps; that is, to consider both the convictions expressed by the
subjects and those expressed by the receivers of the opposed actions.

STEPS 3 AND 4.
THE CONVICTIONS EXPRESSED BY
THE SUBJECTS AND RECEIVERS OF
OPPOSED ACTIONS IN JOHN 4:4-42

As we proceed, let us keep in mind that opposed subjects in a polemical dialogue are primarily contrasted by what they say; they know
what they are talking about!

---

1. The readers are invited to perform step 2, either on their own, or with the help of
the Computer Assisted Lessons (which lead them through the entire process of the structural
exegesis). I am indebted to M. McDaniel and especially to V. Phillips for the interpretation
of John 4. In preparing the corresponding Computer Assisted Lessons, they helped me
greatly in refining my exegesis. One might want to compare our simplified structural exegesis
of John 4 with the detailed structural exegesis of Boers. See Hendrikus Boers, *Neither on
This Mountain nor in Jerusalem: A Study of John 4*, Society of Biblical Literature, Monograph
Series (Atlanta: Scholars Press, 1988).

OPP 4:7-9. Jesus and the Samaritan woman are the subjects of the polemical dialogue. Jesus requests a drink; instead of complying, the woman objects, saying that Jesus should not have made such a request. The Samaritan woman is characterized by her surprise at Jesus' request; it is improper and undesirable, because he is a Jew and she is "a woman of Samaria." According to her, the prohibition (either ethnic or religious prohibition)[2] that "Jews have no dealings[3] with Samaritans" (4:9) should govern Jesus' behavior; it should be what establishes his *will*. The formulation of her response ("of me, a woman of Samaria") signals that this prohibition is also a social prohibition on interaction between a "man" and a "woman." By contrast, Jesus' request makes it clear that he does not abide by this twofold prohibition; his will is not established by it. *For Jesus, interactions between Jews and Samaritans, as well as between men and women, are not improper and undesirable.* This is one of the convictions underscored by this first opposition.

How is the woman's surprise to be interpreted? Does it express that she is in agreement with the prohibition? Several features of the text show that she is not. Both her own statement ("How is it that you, a Jew," 4:9) and the narrator's explanation ("For Jews have no dealings with Samaritans," 4:9) express that this prohibition is a view *of the Jews.*[4] Furthermore, by responding to Jesus (and thus by dealing with him), she shows that she does not abide by the twofold prohibition. As Jesus' will is not established in terms of such a prohibition, so her will is not established in this way, and thus she accepts to enter in dialogue with him. She is surprised, because she discovers that, in this regard, Jesus is like her. But she also displays a misunderstanding of what governs the establishment of Jesus' will; she thinks that it should be governed by the Jewish prohibition. We conclude that the main conviction underscored by this opposition concerns *the way in which Jesus' will is established; it is established by something else than by the Jewish prohibition.*

The woman's misunderstanding concerning Jesus' will is related to her wrong perception of Jesus' identity; for her, he is a Jew like any other Jew. This is one of the points that Jesus underscores in his response to

---

2. At this point we cannot decide if it is a religious or an ethnic prohibition. It will become clear in OPP 4:19-24 that it is a religious prohibition.
3. In the general sense of "no kind of interaction." With Rudolf Schnackenburg, *The Gospel according to John* (New York: Seabury Press, 1980), 425; and Barnabas Lindars, *The Gospel of John,* New Century Bible Commentary (Grand Rapids: Wm. B. Eerdmans; London: Marshall, Morgan & Scott, 1972), 181; but against Raymond E. Brown, *The Gospel according to John I–XII,* Anchor Bible (Garden City, N.Y.: Doubleday & Co., 1966), 170.
4. And more precisely, the view of male Jews. This literary structural observation is in agreement with the historical interpretation that refers to Jewish traditions expressing that Samaritans, and especially Samaritan women, are ritually impure. See Brown, *John I–XII,* 170; Schnackenburg, *John,* 425; Lindars, *John,* 180–81.

her (4:10): She does not know "who it is that is saying to [her], 'Give me a drink.' " Thus the opposition also underscores the conviction that *properly understanding Jesus' identity involves a correct perception of the way in which his will is established.*

As we consider the effect of Jesus' action upon the woman (step 4), we note that the text explains Jesus' request to the woman by mentioning the absence of his disciples (4:8). Thus the woman is asked to play the role that the disciples would have played if they were present. However strange it might appear, Jesus' request puts the woman in the role of a disciple.

OPP 4:10-12. Jesus' reply in 4:10 expresses that, in order to understand why he does not follow the prohibition, the woman needs two kinds of knowledge: knowledge of "the gift of God" and knowledge of "who it is that is" speaking to her. The woman's response in 4:11-12 shows that she lacks these two kinds of knowledge.

We noted that the preceding opposition underscores that the woman is mistaken regarding Jesus' identity. In response to Jesus' words (4:10), she addresses the issue of his identity when she asks, "Are you greater than our father Jacob?" (4:12). The form of this rhetorical question indicates that the woman does *not* think that Jesus is greater than Jacob. Yet in response to Jesus' suggestion that she should have asked a drink from him and that he would have given it to her, she correctly concludes that in such a case Jesus would not be a Jew like any other Jew; he would be greater than Jacob. The effect of her willingness to be in dialogue with Jesus (OPP 4:7-9), and the effect of Jesus' response to her (4:10) is that she envisions the possibility that Jesus may be "greater than Jacob," although she does not believe it.

Furthermore, by stating that Jesus has "nothing to draw with and the well is deep" (4:11), she displays her lack of knowledge of Jesus' *ability* to draw and give water, a knowledge that she would have "if [she] knew the gift of God and who it is that is" speaking to her (4:10). Thus the contrast between Jesus' words and the woman's response underscores that a proper knowledge of Jesus' identity is related to a proper knowledge of his *ability.*[5]

Comparing the first two oppositions, we simply note that the issue of the proper knowledge of Jesus' identity is central in both oppositions. A proper understanding of Jesus' identity involves both a proper knowledge of the way in which his *will* is established, and of his (extraordinary) *ability.*

---

5. The phrases "the gift of God" and "living water" are figures that would need to be explained in step 6 of the exegesis. For a presentation of the main historical critical interpretations, see Brown, *John I–XII,* 178–80.

There also seems to be a difference of understanding regarding the kind of water ("living water") that Jesus would give. This issue is taken up by the following oppositions.

OPP 4:13-15 and 4:13-14. One of the points underscored by the following polemical exchange (OPP 4:13-15) is emphasized by an opposition contained within Jesus' statement: "Every one who drinks of this water will thirst again, but whoever drinks of the water that I shall give will never thirst" (OPP 4:13-14).[6] Since the subjects are indefinite, the points of this latter opposition concern the effects on the receivers (step 4); literal water that quenches physical thirst for a little while is contrasted with living water that quenches spiritual thirst forever as it becomes "a spring of water welling up to eternal life."

Jesus' statement (4:13-14) expresses his *will* to give such spiritual water. By her response in 4:15, the woman shows that she misunderstands Jesus, because she thinks he speaks about literal water. Thus she is mistaken about the nature of Jesus' will (what he wants to give). Despite this misunderstanding, she is characterized by the *will* to receive such water ("give me this water"). *The woman's exclusive concern (what she wants) is what is needed for physical life; while Jesus' concern (what he wants to give) is what is needed for eternal life.* The woman's misunderstanding concerning Jesus' will is related to her inappropriate knowledge of his ability. Here she implicitly acknowledges that he has the ability to give water in a way that is better than Jacob's way of giving water. But she does not yet acknowledge that he has the ability of giving a radically different water, spiritual living water.

Bringing together the points expressed in these oppositions and in the preceding one, we conclude that because of who he is (greater than Jacob), Jesus has both the will and the ability to give water that enables one to have eternal life. The woman's response seems positive: she wants what Jesus offers her (4:15). But she still lacks a proper knowledge of Jesus' identity, of Jesus' will, and of Jesus' ability, because she has an incorrect knowledge of what she really needs.

OPP 4:16-18. Jesus' (apparent) lack of knowledge of the actual marital situation of the woman (4:16, the negative action) is opposed to his detailed knowledge of it expressed in 4:17-18.[7] The point is simply that "despite appearances" Jesus has extraordinary knowledge of her situation. The effect on the woman (receiver, step 4) is expressed at the beginning of

6. This is actually a twofold opposition: drinking "of this water" vs. drinking "of the water I shall give"; thirsting vs. not thirsting.
7. This is a complex opposition between 4:16 (−) "Jesus said to her" and *both* 4:17a (+) "The woman answered" and 4:17b (+) "Jesus said to her, 'You are right. . . .'"

her next response in 4:19 (before she formulates another objection). She has already implicitly acknowledged that Jesus is greater than Jacob in 4:15. Now she acknowledges that he is a prophet, that is, one who has the extraordinary ability to know what is hidden in human situations (and hidden in her answer in 4:17a).

When we compare this opposition with OPP 4:7-9 and its point concerning whether interactions between Jews and Samaritans and men and women are proper or improper, it appears that Jesus' first statement (4:16) fits with the traditional view of men-women relationships held by the Jews according to the woman in 4:9. By giving her the order, "Go, call your husband," Jesus appears to adopt the attitude she expects him to have; the attitude of a Jew for whom his interaction with the woman would be more acceptable if her husband were present. But, if Jesus was a Jew like any other Jew, then he would not know her exact situation: she has had five husbands and now lives with a man who is not her husband (4:18). From the perspective of the value system appealed to in 4:9, she is precisely the kind of woman with whom Jewish men would not want to interact, since her dealings with men are most improper. By demonstrating to her that, during their entire dialogue, he knows her situation, Jesus' response achieves two things. First, it removes any ambiguity regarding the way in which his *will* is established; he does not follow the social prohibition on interaction between men and women. Second, it displays Jesus' knowledge or, more precisely, his extraordinary *ability to know*. Consequently, the woman is given the possibility to progress in her understanding of the identity of Jesus.

We observed that the preceding oppositions (OPP 4:7-9; 4:10-12; 4:13-15) underscored that in order to have a proper knowledge of Jesus' identity one needs to have a proper understanding of his will and extraordinary ability. As a result of this new polemical exchange (OPP 4:16-18), it is now unambiguous that Jesus' will is not established by following *social* prohibitions on interaction between men and women. Thus the woman has progressed in her knowledge of Jesus' will; yet it is not yet clear for her whether or not Jesus follows the ethnic or religious prohibition on interaction between Jews and Samaritans. This issue will be taken up by the next polemical exchange. As another and more directly significant result of this polemical exchange, the woman has now a clear perception of Jesus' extraordinary ability; it is an extraordinary *ability to know*. With this newly acquired knowledge regarding Jesus' ability, the woman is in a position to reach a better understanding of his identity: "I perceive that you are a prophet" (4:19).

These observations on the correlations posited by the text and on the pattern formed by these oppositions are confirmed by 4:19-20, where the other part of the prohibition (regarding the interaction between Jews and Samaritans) is taken up.

OPP 4:19-24 and 4:22.   When we compare the statement of the woman (4:20) and Jesus' response (4:21-24), the convictions underscored by this polemical dialogue are easily identified; they concern worship as that which separates Samaritans from Jews. This point is further emphasized by a secondary opposition (OPP 4:22).[8]

The woman now recognizes that Jesus is a prophet. But, for her, this means that he is a *Jewish* servant of God, as is expressed by her statement in 4:20 which shows that she expects him to abide by the religious[9] prohibition that Jews and Samaritans should remain separated because of their different views concerning worship. A part of Jesus' answer acknowledges that this religious prohibition has its origin with the Jews: "You worship what you do not know; we worship what we know, for salvation is from the Jews" (4:22). This statement emphatically emphasizes (by means of the secondary opposition it contains) that the Samaritan woman misunderstands the reasons for the prohibition on religious interaction between Jews and Samaritans. She expresses that Samaritans and Jews should remain separated because they worship in different places, and justifies her implicit claim that Samaritans worship at the right place by saying, "Our fathers worshiped on this mountain." For her, the proper way of worshiping is perceived in terms of the *place* of worship and in terms of the *past*. By contrast, Jesus' reference to the Jewish view ("we") of the religious prohibition underscores that true worship must be based on *a knowledge of who is worshiped*. Since the Jews ("we") have this knowledge and the Samaritans do not, the Jews are in a privileged position ("salvation is from the Jews"). Does this mean that Jesus follows the religious prohibition separating Jews from Samaritans, as the woman expects? The contrasts between the rest of his answer and the woman's claims make it clear that he does not.

Against the woman's claim that proper worship is conceived in terms of the *place* of worship, Jesus affirms that the place of worship is irrelevant (4:21). Against her claim that proper worship is conceived in terms of the *past*, he affirms that true worship is to be conceived in terms of the *future* ("the hour is coming," 4:21, 23), which is actually *present* ("and now is," 4:23). Furthermore, the concluding phrase of 4:23, "such the Father seeks to worship him" suggests that the Jews are not yet the ideal worshipers. Although the Jews know whom they worship, they do not take into account

---

8. Once again it is a twofold opposition: worshiping an unknown God vs. worshiping a known God; not knowing vs. knowing.

9. It is now clear that it is a *religious* prohibition, and not an ethnic prohibition.

the true nature of God, which is that "God is spirit" (4:24). This knowledge of the nature of God (that the Jews do not yet have) gives the worshipers the *ability* (the know-how) to worship correctly, that is, "in spirit and in truth" (4:23). In addition, the knowledge of the nature of God should establish the *will* to worship in this proper way ("those who worship him *must* worship him in spirit and truth," 4:24).

In sum, the convictions expressed by this opposition are that proper worship can be practiced (1) if one understands worship in terms of *time* rather than in terms of space, the *place* of worship; (2) if one has a proper understanding of the *present* (now) as the time in which the eschatological time (the future) already erupts (4:23); and (3) if one has a proper understanding of the nature of God (that "God is spirit," 4:24). In addition, this opposition expresses the conviction that the knowledge of the nature of God establishes both the ability and the will of true worshipers.

For the woman, the effect of Jesus' statement (step 4) is to communicate to her radically new knowledge about worship that challenges her traditional Samaritan understanding of worship based on the tradition passed down from "our fathers" (4:20). For her, this raises once again (cf. 4:12) the issue of whether or not Jesus has a greater authority than the fathers—the issue of Jesus' identity as related to his ability. Furthermore, if she accepts Jesus' view of worship, then she will have to acknowledge that Jesus' will is not established on the basis of the religious prohibition on interaction between Samaritans and Jews, since all are supposed to worship in the same way, "in spirit and in truth" (4:23-24). Rather, his will is established on the basis of his knowledge of the nature of God, as should be the case for the will of any true worshiper.

OPP 4:25-26. In this last polemical exchange between the woman and Jesus, since the woman's statement is an answer to Jesus' words, the things the Messiah reveals (in the future for the woman, 4:25) are nothing other than the knowledge that will make people able and willing to "worship in spirit and in truth," namely, the knowledge that "God is spirit." Thus she affirms that the role of the Messiah is to reveal the nature of God, a point that Jesus does not reject in any way by his answer (4:26). What is wrong with her point of view is once again the timing and her lack of knowledge of who it is that is speaking to her. While she speaks of a future Messiah, Jesus presents himself, in the present, as the Messiah (4:26).

The following verses (4:28-29, that do not include oppositions) express the effect of Jesus' answer upon her; she goes into the city and says, "Come see a man who told me all that I ever did. Can this be the Christ?" Thus she entertains the possibility that Jesus might be the Messiah.

At the conclusion of the polemical dialogue between Jesus and the woman, we summarize our findings. We noted the progressive dismantling of the woman's expectations that Jesus, a Jewish man, would not want to associate with her, a Samaritan and a woman. Jesus successively shows that his will is established neither on the basis of the Jewish social prohibition on interaction between the sexes (OPP 4:16-18), nor on the basis of the religious prohibition on interaction between Jews and Samaritans (OPP 4:19-24). Rather, Jesus' will is established on the basis of his knowledge of the nature of God. In a parallel movement, the woman's level of understanding of Jesus progressively increases as the dialogue proceeds. First, despite misconceptions about the nature of the "water," she acknowledges Jesus' ability to give "living water," thereby tentatively making Jesus "greater than Jacob." Second, she perceives that he is a "prophet," because of his extraordinary ability to know hidden situations. Finally, she realizes that he might be the Messiah.

Some Additional Observations on John 4:27-30. Although 4:27-30 does not contain any opposition (and thus should be studied in step 6), a few remarks about these verses are necessary because of the qualifications they provide for the disciples who are the polemical interlocutors of Jesus in the following oppositions. These verses weave together statements about the disciples (4:27) and about the woman (4:28-30), thereby inviting the readers to compare the disciples and the woman. Reading 4:27 in this perspective, it appears that, as the woman is surprised by the fact that Jesus does not abide by the Jewish social and religious prohibition on interaction between a Jewish man and a Samaritan woman, so the disciples are surprised ("marveled") "that he was talking with a woman." The formulation of their question, "Why are you talking with her?" shows that they share the expectation that the woman had at the beginning of her dialogue with Jesus. Yet the text also mentions that the disciples do not voice their objection to Jesus' behavior ("but none said"). This attitude shows that they acknowledge his authority more than the woman does. For the readers, the disciples' relationship with Jesus has been established earlier in the Gospel, where they acknowledged Jesus as the Christ, Messiah, Son of God (see 1:41, 45, 49). Indeed, one of the disciples, Nathanael, came to believe because Jesus told him what he had been doing (1:48-50), as the woman tentatively expressed her belief that Jesus is the Christ because he "told me all that I ever did" (4:29). Thus, 4:27-30 shows that the disciples, who replace the woman as polemical partners with Jesus, are like the woman in that they think that Jesus should find it improper to interact with a woman and in that they believe that Jesus is the Messiah. Although their belief is less tentative than the woman's, we can expect that just as the woman lacked knowledge, so do the disciples. The text invites us to compare the polemical dialogues between the woman and Jesus and between the disciples and Jesus.

OPP 4:31-32. By urging Jesus to eat, the disciples give him a respectful order—an attempt to establish Jesus' will. By his answer, Jesus refuses to have his will changed; he asserts it. Consequently, the statement, "I have food which you do not know," shows that the disciples lack knowledge not only concerning food, but also, and more fundamentally, concerning Jesus' will.

OPP 4:33-34. This new opposition underscores that the disciples misunderstand what Jesus said about food, as the woman misunderstood what he said about water. Like the woman, the disciples are preoccupied with physical needs over spiritual needs. When Jesus says "eating food," they fail to recognize that Jesus speaks about doing "the will of him who sent him" (4:34). Thus, together with OPP 4:31-32, this opposition underscores the importance of knowing Jesus' *will*, a will to do the *will of God*. Since this involves a doing whose end is accomplishing God's work (4:34), we can say that eating the food unknown to the disciples constitutes Jesus' *vocation*. In order to understand Jesus' vocation, the disciples need to know (1) the relationship of Jesus with God (God sent Jesus) and (2) what God's will is.

As we consider the correlations posited by the text between these oppositions and preceding ones, we note that OPP 4:19-24 also deals with the proper understanding of a "vocation": worshiping "in spirit and in truth" is what believers should do; it is doing the will of God. Note that in each case a proper understanding of the vocation (of Jesus, of the believers) involves knowing something about God. In order to have a proper understanding of worshiping, one needs to know that "God is spirit" (4:24). In order to understand his vocation properly, Jesus needs to know that God is the one who sent him. Thus, we can suspect that, as the knowledge of God's nature is a condition for the believers' knowledge of the will of God, so the knowledge of God's relationship with him is a condition for Jesus' knowledge of the will of God. In other words, the knowledge that God sent him gives Jesus the ability to know and the will to do the will of God.

OPP 4:35-38. This is the last opposition of the discourse unit. In 4:35a, Jesus suggests what the disciples would reply to his preceding statement, "There are yet four months, then comes the harvest,"[10] a reply to which he objects (4:35b-38). We first note that the theme of 4:35, harvest, is the process of gathering food, the theme of 4:33-34. We are not surprised that as the disciples speak about physical food (4:33) while Jesus refers to

---

10. Possibly a reference to the length of time between sowing and harvesting, that might have been a proverb. See Brown, *John I–XII*, 182; Schnackenburg, *John*, 448–49.

spiritual food (4:34), so here the disciples (hypothetically) speak about physical harvesting, while Jesus refers to spiritual harvesting. This correspondence is even more apparent when we note that Jesus' food is an activity ("My food is *to do* the will of him who sent me," 4:34) as harvesting is; indeed, these two words designate the same activity. (Thus in 4:36 Jesus is the harvester and God is the sower.) But the primary contrast between the two statements in 4:35a and 35b concerns *time*. For the disciples, harvesting should take place in the future (in four months). For Jesus, now is the time for harvesting, since "the fields are already white for harvest." Considering the effect of these words on the receivers, it appears that a full-fledged disciple—who properly understands "who" Jesus is, his vocation, and the will of God—needs to know that the present is a very special time: it is the time when the harvest is ready, as it is the time when a true kind of worship can take place (OPP 4:19-24) and when the Messiah has come (OPP 4:25-26).

The rest of Jesus' response (4:36-38) shifts the emphasis to the harvesters (or reapers). Jesus has told the disciples, "I sent you to reap" (4:38). In other words, he has given them a vocation similar to his own (he is the harvester in 4:36). He has given them the vocation of harvesting. Or, since "harvesting" and "food" are equivalent, he has given them "food," a food/harvesting that results in receiving "wages," themselves certainly related to eternal life (4:36). Thus, as Jesus the harvester rejoices with God the sower (4:36), so the disciples who are made harvesters by Jesus who sent them (4:38) are in a position to rejoice with the sowers (God, Jesus, other people) as they participate in gathering "fruit for eternal life."

When this is recognized, a comparison with OPP 4:13-14 becomes possible and shows that "food/harvesting" and "living water" are functionally identical, since both are given by Jesus, and since both have eternal life as an ultimate result. It should follow that by offering water to the woman, Jesus also offered her a vocation identical to that of the disciples, and similar to his own. But is this conclusion valid? To see that it is, we need to understand more precisely what is the vocation of spiritual harvesting that the disciples and the woman should perform with Jesus. In fact, the text expresses it in its concluding verses, 4:39-42; we need to relate these with what precedes.

In 4:32 Jesus said, "I have food to eat." Since his food is doing the will of God, it means that Jesus is in the process of doing something. What is he doing? He spoke to the Samaritan woman, who has now gone to the city suggesting that Jesus might be the Christ (4:29), and the people of the city "were coming to him" (4:30). Thus, through the intermediary of the woman, Jesus is doing something for these Samaritans. This is further specified in 4:39-42. "Many Samaritans from that city believed in him because of the woman's testimony" (4:39). He stays with them at their request; thus, the separation of Jesus from the Samaritans (Jesus sitting at the well outside the city, 4:6, cf. 4:9) is overcome. As a result, "many more believed because of his word" (4:41); they believe that he is "the Savior of the world" (4:42). Using the metaphor of the preceding verses, we can say that the people of the city have been harvested. We recognize three steps in this process of harvesting, and we note who performed them:

1. Bringing people (or causing people to go) to Jesus; this is what the woman achieved by her testimony (4:28-30);
2. Helping people to believe in a preliminary way that Jesus is the Christ; this is partly achieved by the woman's testimony (4:39) and partly achieved by Jesus' own words (4:41);
3. Causing people to believe fully in Jesus as the Savior of the world; this is achieved by Jesus and Jesus alone (4:42).

We conclude that the harvesting of the people of the city is performed by Jesus and the woman. Note the complementarity of Jesus' and the woman's actions. The woman brings people to Jesus by her testimony, "he told me all that I ever did" (4:29, 39). Some have a partial belief because of her testimony (4:39), while others do not (cf. 4:41). Yet, all have full belief only when they are directly in Jesus' presence and hear his words (4:42). Ironically, the disciples who had been given this vocation (4:38) produce no harvest. Even though they go to the city (4:8), they fail to bring anyone to Jesus. *The Samaritan woman is presented as an ideal disciple fulfilling her vocation of harvesting* (we noted that 4:8 already suggests that she is playing the role of the disciples).

When has the Samaritan woman received such a vocation? Actually, one could raise the same question about the disciples.[11] But when one remembers that "living water" and "food/harvesting" are functionally identical, it appears that she has received this vocation through her dialogue with Jesus. Despite appearances, she has received water, the vocation to harvest, since she was motivated to perform this vocation. Certainly, the central moment of her dialogue with Jesus, what motivated her to believe, was when, in her words, "he told me all that I ever did" (4:29, 39); that is, when she tentatively recognized who he is, a prophet, the Messiah. This belief in Jesus as prophet, as Messiah (knowing who he is, 4:10) opened the possibility for her to receive the "water" that he offered her. But what did she receive from Jesus? Besides the knowledge

---

11. The commentators note that there is no mention before 4:38 that Jesus has sent or commissioned the disciples to go in mission, and make proposals to explain this discrepancy. Cf. Brown, *John I–XII*, 183; Schnackenburg, *John*, 452–53.

of Jesus' identity, there is only one thing that she did not know (4:22) and that Jesus made known to her; namely, that God is Spirit, a knowledge that should motivate ("must") believers to "worship in spirit and truth" (4:24). This revelation of the nature of God is the water which is also a call to do the will of God, a vocation to harvest.[12]

STEP 5.
THE PATTERN OF
THE SYSTEM OF CONVICTIONS
EXPRESSED IN JOHN 4:4-42

From the above discussion, it is clear that most of the convictions underscored by the oppositions of actions of John 4:4-42 concern believers (among whom the woman and the disciples) and their relationship to Jesus as mediator. This is confirmed by noting that the theme of the discourse unit, as expressed by the inverted parallelisms between 4:4-10 and 4:39-42, concerns the transformation of an original situation in which (1) Jesus is separated from the Samaritans of the city of Sychar, and (2) Jesus is not known by the woman who thinks he is a Jew like any other Jew (4:10; the other Samaritans do not even know that he is at the well). This original situation is transformed into a final situation in which Jesus is united with the Samaritans who believe and know that he is the Savior. Thus, there are two main categories of convictions: (1) convictions about believers and their relations (or lack of relations) to Jesus, and (2) convictions about the mediator and his identity (knowing or not that he is the Messiah, the Savior).[13] We begin by establishing the hierarchy of convictions about Jesus as mediator.

The Hierarchy of Convictions about Jesus.   In our study of the oppositions, we noted that Jesus is characterized by:

— His will to interact with the Samaritan woman, even though she is a woman and a Samaritan (OPP 4:7-9);

— His knowledge of the gift of God and of who he is (OPP 4:10-12);

— His will and ability to give "living water" "welling up to eternal life" (OPP 4:10-12; 4:13-15) and to cause people to believe (4:41-42);

— His ability to know and expose hidden human situations (OPP 4:16-18);

---

12. We can now understand why there is no earlier mention of the sending of the disciples. For John, as a result of believing in Jesus, they received his testimony about the nature of God, and thus they received a vocation. In agreement with Lindars, *John*, 197.

13. There are also a few convictions about the divine. The woman (and potentially the disciples) might also belong to the category "religious leaders." But the text does not allow us to make a clear distinction between religious leaders and believers.

— His knowledge of the nature of God, of time (the Messianic time is now), and of true worship (OPP 4:19-24; see OPP 4:35-38);

— His knowledge of the will of God and his will to do the will of God (OPP 4:31-32, 4:33-34);

— His knowledge that he is sent by God (OPP 4:33-34);

— His authority to send harvesters/disciples who are then in a position to share the joy of the sower (OPP 4:35-38).

As such, Jesus is "greater than Jacob" (4:11-14), a "prophet" (4:19), the Messiah or Christ (4:25-26), the "Savior of the world" (4:42). These convictions can be organized in the following hierarchy:

1. Jesus is sent by God (4:34);
2. He has knowledge of the nature of God, of time, and of the will of God (4:19-24, 35-38) (this is during his ministry, and thus after he has been sent by God);
3. He has the will to do God's will, as well as the ability and authority to do it (4:31-32) (we noted that the establishment of Jesus' will is based upon his knowledge of the nature and will of God, rather than on social and religious prohibitions);
4. He does it (A) by exposing hidden human situations (4:17-18), causing people to believe in him (4:29, 41); (B) by giving people "living water" (4:10-15; cf. 4:7-26), causing people to go and bear testimony, as well as by sending disciples (4:38);
5. In the process, he gives them access to eternal life (4:14) and to sharing the joy of the sower (4:36).[14]

The Hierarchy of Convictions about Believers. The hierarchy of the convictions about believers can be established without first listing all the convictions we discovered in our study of the oppositions. This can be done if we reflect from the end of the hierarchy toward its beginning (a procedure that is often convenient). We number this hierarchy in reverse order to facilitate the comparison with the hierarchy of John 3:1-21 (it is printed in the right order below).

— (7) The ultimate good is eternal life (4:14, 36) and/or joy shared with the sower (God, 4:36).

The condition for obtaining eternal life or joy with God is:

— (6) Fulfilling (A) the vocation of harvesting, as the woman did by her testimony (4:29, 39). It involves leaving Jesus, as well as leaving

---

14. Because of the correspondence between "living water welling up to eternal life" and "food/harvesting fruit for eternal life," the harvesters' wages and their rejoicing together with the sower (4:36) signify that the harvesters themselves participate in eternal life.

"her water jar" (4:28); that is, forgoing one's pursuit of the satisfaction of one's physical needs (4:13-15, 31-34). (B) Another part of this vocation is worshiping God "in spirit and truth" (4:24).

It is not clear in 4:4-42 how these two parts of the believers' vocation are hierarchically interrelated, although we can suspect that "worshiping in spirit and in truth" (B) might be a necessary preparation for "harvesting" (A). Regarding the latter, we have interpreted "the woman left her water jar" (4:28) as a figurative expression of one of the convictions expressed in 4:13-15 and in 4:31-34; namely, the conviction that, by contrast with the woman in 4:15 and the disciples in 4:31, 33, faithful believers and Jesus forgo the pursuit of the satisfaction of physical needs (for literal water and food).

The preceding stage of the hierarchy appears when we note that the evil corresponding to fulfilling the vocation of harvesting is not doing it, as exemplified by the disciples' behavior. Why did they not do it? As OPP 4:31-32 and 4:33-34 underscore, it is because the disciples do not know the will of God ("food") that Jesus carries out and that they should also carry out as harvesters sent by him (4:38). Thus, the condition for carrying out this vocation and for being willing to do it is:

— (5) Receiving from Jesus a knowledge of the will of God (this amounts to receiving a vocation [being sent to reap, 4:38], "food" [4:32], "living water" [4:10, 13-14] that those who think in terms of physical needs to do not know); receiving a knowledge of the nature of God (that "God is spirit," 4:24).

The woman in OPP 4:10-11 exemplifies a person who is not receiving living water, the knowledge of the will of God. This is so because she does not know who Jesus is and what his ability is, and because she thinks that he is a Jew like any other Jew who abides by the Jewish prohibitions. Thus, as is further expressed by OPP 4:25-26, the positive condition for receiving from Jesus a knowledge of the will of God is:

— (4) Knowing who Jesus is, namely, the Messiah, the Christ (4:25-26), the Savior of the world (4:42); that is, believing in him (4:39). This involves knowing that now is the time of the Messiah (4:25-26), and thus the time of the harvest (4:35) or of salvation.

As 4:39-42 expresses, to have a full knowledge of who Jesus is one needs to be in the presence of Jesus, to interact with him, as the woman did (4:7-26), and as other Samaritans do (4:40). Thus, the condition for knowing Jesus is:

— (3) Coming to Jesus and interacting with him, as the woman (4:7-26) and the people of the city (4:30, 40) do.

Note that as they are coming to Jesus, some already have a tentative belief (cf. 4:39 and 4:42) because of the woman's testimony, while others do not yet have belief (4:41). As the latter came to Jesus for other reasons (e.g., curiosity or simply to be with the rest of the people) than belief, so the woman originally came to Jesus simply because she was going to draw water from the well (4:7). She was nevertheless willing to interact with him (although she was surprised that he wanted to interact with her). The condition for coming/interacting with Jesus is:

— (2) Being willing to come/interact with Jesus (4:30).

Being willing to come/interact with Jesus demands that whatever prevents it be overcome, including not only a simple lack of knowledge of his presence (the case of the people of the city), but also social separation (between men and women) and religious separation (between Jews and Samaritans). The first kind of obstacle is overcome by the woman's testimony. The second kind of obstacle, which would have potentially prevented interaction between Jesus and the woman, had been overcome before their encounter. To the woman's surprise, Jesus does not abide by the Jewish social and religious prohibitions (OPP 4:7-9); thus she discovers that Jesus does not put any obstacle to interactions with him. But neither does the woman; she already has the same attitude as Jesus vis-à-vis social and religious prohibitions on interactions. Thus there are alternative conditions for being willing to come/interact with Jesus:

— (1) Either receiving the testimony of a believer/disciple about what Jesus did to bring her/him to belief ("He told me all that I ever did," 4:29, 39),[15] or sharing Jesus' attitude against social and religious separation (4:7-26).

CONCLUSION:
A COMPARISON OF
THE PATTERNS OF CONVICTIONS
IN JOHN 4:4-42 AND JOHN 3:1-21

Obviously, our structural exegesis of John 4:4-42 is not complete. We would need to proceed to the study of the specific features of the discourse unit (step 6) by clarifying the many figures this unit involves in the process of elucidating its discursive strategy. But the results of the first five steps of the exegesis have already established the characteristic faith-pattern expressed by this text, a faith-pattern that we can compare with that of other texts.

As we compare the above hierarchies of the convictions about Jesus and believers elucidated by our study of John 4:4-42 (purposefully considered in and of itself) with those elucidated by our study of John 3:1-21 (see chap. 3), it soon appears that they are quite similar, but not identical.

15. Note that this testimony can be quite tentative: "Can this be the Christ?" (4:29).

So as to facilitate our comparison of the hierarchies of convictions about Jesus, we reproduce the two hierarchies side by side.

John 3:1-21	John 4:4-42
1. Jesus is in heaven (3:11) and has firsthand knowledge of heavenly things (3:16-17);	
2. Jesus is sent into the world, descends from heaven (3:16-17);	1. Jesus is sent by God (4:34);
3. Jesus is thus able to bear witness not only about earthly things but also about heavenly things (3:11-12); Jesus is light of the world (3:20-21) and true teacher (3:4-5);	2. He has knowledge of the nature of God, of time, and of the will of God (4:19-24; 35-38);
	3. He has the will to do God's will, as well as the ability and authority to do it (4:31-32);
	4. He does it (A) exposing hidden human situations (4:17-18), causing people to believe in him (4:29, 41); (B) by giving people living water (4:10-15; cf. 4:7-26), causing people to go and bear testimony, as well as by sending disciples (4:38);
4. Jesus ascended to heaven (3:13) because he must be lifted up (3:14);	
5. Jesus gives eternal life to people.	5. In the process, he gives them access to eternal life (4:14) and to sharing the joy of the sower (4:36).

As our way of printing these hierarchies attempts to show, the convictions about "Jesus being in heaven" and "Jesus ascending to heaven" (convictions 1 and 4 of the hierarchy in 3:1-21) are not expressed in 4:4-42. Yet, the former is presupposed by the conviction that Jesus was sent by God, found in both passages. Conversely, the convictions concerning the qualifications of Jesus in his role as mediator are much more detailed in 4:4-42 than in 3:1-21 (2, 3, 4 in the hierarchy of 4:4-42 correspond to 3 in that of John 3:1-21). They nevertheless correspond to each other. John 3:1-21 emphasizes the origin of Jesus' knowledge of God (Jesus knows heavenly things, and thus God, because he was in heaven); 4:4-42 stresses that Jesus has this knowledge during his ministry. The other qualifications merely specify those expressed in 3:1-21 (conviction 3). In sum, as we anticipated, each discourse unit emphasizes certain convictions about Jesus, but the pattern is clearly the same. Jesus offers the possibility of eternal life (joy with God) to people, because he and he alone has all the qualifications required to transmit to them the knowledge of God, and he has all these qualifications because he is sent by God (and thus come from heaven).

Let us compare the hierarchies of the convictions about believers.

John 3:1-21	John 4:4-42
1. Would-be believers are in God and have (some) truth (3:21); 2. They do "what is true" (3:21);	1. Either receiving the testimony of a believer/disciple about what Jesus did to bring her/him to belief (4:29, 39), or sharing Jesus' attitude against social separations (4:7-26);
3. They are willing to come to the light (that reveals the true character of their deeds, 3:19-21);	2. Being willing to come/interact with Jesus; 3. Coming to Jesus and interacting with him, as the woman did (4:7-26), and as the people of the city did (4:30, 40);
4. They believe in Jesus, in the name of the only Son (3:18; they recognize that he truly is the light, because he reveals the true character of their deeds, 3:19-21);	4. Knowing who Jesus is, namely, the Messiah, the Christ (4:25-26), the Savior of the world (4:42), that is, believing in him (4:39). This involves knowing that now is the time of the Messiah (4:25-26), and thus the time of the harvest (4:35) or of salvation;
5. They believe (receive) Jesus' testimony (since they acknowledge him as the only Son, the light, they can trust his testimony, 3:11b-12, 18); 6. They are born of the Spirit (and thus are spirit, and have the will to come from, and go to, places unknown to other people, 3:5-8);	5. Receiving from Jesus a knowledge of the will of God (this amounts to receiving a vocation [being sent to reap, 4:38], food [4:32], living water [4:10, 13-14] that those who think in terms of physical needs do not know); receiving a knowledge of the nature of God (that "God is spirit," 4:24);
7. Then they have firsthand knowledge and are in a position to bear witness to the role of the Spirit in people being born anew (to bear witness to earthly things), and thus to be a true "teacher of Israel" (3:10-12);	6. Fulfilling one's vocation: (A) Harvesting, as the woman did by her testimony (4:29, 39). It involves leaving Jesus, as well as leaving "her water jar" (4:28); that is, forgoing one's pursuit of the satisfaction of one's physical needs (4:13-15, 31-34). (B) Worshiping God "in spirit and truth" (4:24);
8. They can enter the kingdom of God (3:5) and have eternal life (3:15-16), the ultimate good.	7. The ultimate good is "eternal life" (4:14, 36) and/or joy with the sower (4:36).

Concerning the hierarchies of convictions about believers found in John 3:1-21 and 4:4-42, we also find differences regarding specific convictions, but a similar pattern. The last convictions of the hierarchies (8 and 7, respectively) are identical. The preceding sets of convictions (5, 6, and 7 in 3:1-21, and 5 and 6 in 4:4-42) appear to be different. In considering these convictions more closely, one recognizes the same pattern. In both cases, the vocation of the believers is to bear witness to what the Spirit (3:1-21) or Jesus (4:4-42) has done for believers. But for this, believers need to be "born of the Spirit" (3:1-21) or to worship God "in spirit and truth" (4:4-42); these two convictions are closely related. Once again, the *origin* of the qualifications (for performing one's vocation one needs to be born of Spirit) is emphasized in 3:1-21; while 4:4-42 stresses the vocation itself and its fulfillment (one must worship in spirit). For this, in both cases, one needs to have received and to believe Jesus' testimony; its content is specified in 4:4-42—it includes a knowledge of God's nature and of God's will. For this, one needs to believe in Jesus (4 in 3:1-21); that is, to know who Jesus is (4 in 4:4-42), knowledge that one truly has only after having come to Jesus (3 in 3:1-21, and 2 and 3 in 4:4-42). The first conviction in John 4:4-42 and the first two convictions in the hierarchy of John 3:1-21, that should correspond to each other, do not seem to do so. In 3:1-21, it seemed that only good doers could come to Jesus (the light). Yet, let us remember that 3:21 speaks of doing what is true and of deeds wrought in God, phrases that are far from being clear despite the oppositions. In light of 4:4-42, it appears that people who receive the testimony of a believer would have some truth and would then be doing what is true. The case of the woman is even more significant. In one sense, one could say that, rather than being a good doer, she is an evil doer, since she lives with a man who is not her husband (4:18). But this would be evaluating the woman according to the system of values implied in 4:9 and rejected by Jesus! Actually, as is underscored by the oppositions, the woman has the same attitude against social separations that Jesus has. Her interacting with Jesus beyond social and religious prohibitions is doing what is true, a deed wrought in God who should be worshiped by all people without distinction because he is spirit. Thus there are two ways through which one starts on the road toward belief and discipleship: either by means of the testimony of a believer, or because one already has something (an attitude) in common with Jesus (doing what is true, deeds wrought in God).

In sum, although certain convictions are expressed in somewhat different ways, we can conclude that the pattern of convictions about believers in the two discourse units is the same. Because of preliminary knowledge of the truth, that one has on one's own or that one received through the testimony of a believer, people do what is true; they have the will to come to Jesus; they believe in him; they receive his teachings (about God and his will); then, they are equipped with the knowledge necessary to worship in spirit and truth and are born of the Spirit; they carry out a vocation that leads them to go to unexpected places (leaving behind what they need to satisfy physical needs); and, ultimately, they receive eternal life.

These observations are enough to confirm that by studying any given discourse unit of a text, one elucidates the basic pattern of its system of convictions, even though each unit underscores specific convictions related to its theme. The study of a few discourse units is often helpful for refining one's understanding of this pattern.

5

Second Exercise in
Structural Exegesis:
Luke 10:21-42

We now turn to a discourse unit with a different literary character. Luke 10:21-42 is made up of apparently unrelated pericopes[1] that seem to be juxtaposed with each other and includes a section containing an embedded parable—two frequent phenomena in the Gospels. This choice simultaneously allows us to show how the structural exegesis of such a passage is performed and to elucidate basic characteristics of Luke's faith—the pattern of his system of convictions. Our first task is to establish that Luke 10:21-42 is a complete discourse unit.

STEP 1.
LUKE 10:21-42 AS
A COMPLETE DISCOURSE UNIT

As we read this passage, it soon appears that Luke 10:25-37 forms a complete discourse unit or sub-unit of the Gospel according to Luke. Note that 10:25 introduces a new character in the story, the lawyer, who disappears after the end of the dialogue in 10:37. Note the inverted parallelism between 10:25 ("What shall I do?") and 10:37, where Jesus says, "Go and do likewise," a more complete answer than the one found in 10:28. As we consider the preceding and following verses, however, it becomes clear that 10:25-37 is a sub-unit of a larger discourse unit.

Luke 10:25-37 is surrounded by short pericopes (10:21-22; 23-24; 38-42) that do not belong to the preceding (9:51—10:20) and the following

---

1. Source criticism points out that two of these pericopes (short self-contained passages) are from the source Q (Luke 10:21-22, 23-24; cf. Matt. 11:25-27; 13:16-17), that another is somewhat parallel to Mark and Matthew (Luke 10:25-28; Mark 12:28-34; Matt. 22:35-40), while the others (Luke 10:29-37, 38-42) are peculiar to Luke.

(11:1-13) discourse units. We find a strong sign that a unit ends in 10:42 in that 11:1 is the clear beginning of a discourse unit about prayer which ends in 11:13.[2] Since it has nothing to do with prayer, 10:38-42, the story of Martha and Mary, does not belong to this unit, and thus certainly belongs with 10:25-37.

Where does the unit that ends in 10:42 begin? First we must demonstrate that 10:21-24 belong to this unit rather than to the preceding one. As Charles H. Talbert argues, the preceding unit begins in 9:51 and is composed of several sub-units, the first one, 9:51-56 (the unsuccessful sending of messengers to a Samaritan village), forming inverted parallelisms with the concluding one (the successful sending of the seventy in mission).[3] This latter sub-unit that begins in 10:1 is concluded by 10:17-20 (the return of the seventy), as is shown by the inverted parallelisms formed by 10:18-20, Jesus' response to the seventy's joyful exclamation, with 10:1-3 (showing that the sub-unit is complete) and with 9:51-56 (showing that the unit is complete).[4] A second sign that a new unit begins with 10:21-24 is that these verses introduce new themes: things hidden from the wise and revealed to the babes, the mutual knowledge of Father and Son, and the disciples who see and hear what prophets and kings desired to see. I do not deny that 10:21-24 is closely linked with the preceding unit;[5] it is a kind of reflection on the implications of the mission of the seventy. Yet the introduction of new themes in the form of an interpretation of the significance of a preceding unit is a common way of introducing a new discourse unit. In sum, these observations concerning the inverted parallelisms of the following and preceding units and their themes suggest that 10:21-42 is a complete discourse unit. Yet we cannot

2. With Charles H. Talbert, *Reading Luke: A Literary and Theological Commentary on the Third Gospel* (New York: Crossroad, 1982), 127–34.

3. As Talbert argues (*Reading Luke*, 114–19). I agree that the unit begins in 9:51, but I disagree with Talbert regarding its ending. He considers the inclusions, but he does not take into account the inverted parallelisms, which demand that the unit ends at 10:20, not 10:24.

4. Both 9:51-56 and 10:17-20 mention apocalyptic destructions of evil. In 9:54-55 the disciples are rebuked by Jesus for wanting to bring this destruction upon the Samaritan village; in 10:18-19 Jesus saw "Satan fall like lightning from heaven" and the disciples are described as having been given authority over all the power of the enemy. By contrast, 10:21-24 does not form any inverted parallelisms with either 10:13 or 9:51-56. Thus we cannot accept Talbert's suggestion regarding the end of this unit.

5. The temporal phrase "in that same hour" (10:21) both ties together (as Talbert and other commentators emphasize) and *separates* what follows and the preceding verses. It signals that 10:21ff interprets the significance of the mission of the seventy and its outcome (10:1-20). Yet, it also marks that the following verses deal with a new issue or theme; if these verses had further unfolded the previous theme, there would not be any need for a temporal marker! Despite a certain continuity in themes (the themes of "rejoicing," 10:17, 20; 10:21; of the Samaritans and their relations to Jews, 9:51-55; 10:30-37), a new discourse unit begins in 10:21.

definitely conclude that this is the case as long as we have not identified clear inverted parallelisms between its beginning and end.

Comparing 10:21-24 and 10:38-42, we discover that they do form inverted parallelisms. In 10:21-24 the wise and understanding from whom things are hidden are contrasted with the babes and disciples to whom things are revealed by Jesus and who are declared blessed because they see and hear. In 10:38-42 Martha, who "was distracted with much serving" and does not listen to Jesus' teaching, is contrasted with Mary, who listens to Jesus' teaching and is declared to have "chosen the good portion." The parallelisms appear: Martha is both like and unlike the wise and understanding—she is deprived of knowledge as they are, although she serves Jesus and is in dialogue with him (there is hope for her); similarly, Mary is both like and unlike the babes and disciples—she receives a revelation from Jesus, although she is not a baby, nor formally speaking a disciple (she has not gone into mission).[6] Thus we conclude that these inverted parallelisms express a theme that concerns those who receive or do not receive Jesus' teaching-revelation (further see step 5 below). Thus, Luke 10:21-42 forms a complete unit, as our study of the oppositions will further confirm.

STEPS 2, 3, AND 4.
IDENTIFICATION OF THE CONVICTIONS
EXPRESSED IN LUKE 10:21-42[7]

We successively consider the oppositions of actions in the introductory verses (10:21-24), the dialogue between Jesus and the lawyer (10:25-29; 36-37), the parable of the Good Samaritan (10:30-35), and the story of Martha and Mary (10:38-42).

The Introductory Verses (Luke 10:21-24)

OPP 10:22a. A first opposition[8] is found in the elliptic phrase "no one knows who the Son is except the Father." It contrasts God and human beings in terms of their respective relationship to Jesus. Alone the One

6. If we compare 10:38-42 with 10:25-29 (the introduction of a unit beginning in 10:25 as proposed by Talbert), then the only potential inverted parallelism would be between the lawyer calling Jesus "teacher" and Mary sitting at the feet of Jesus (as one sits at the feet of one's teacher). This is noteworthy, but not sufficient for arguing that the unit begins in 10:25.

7. In order to be concise we simultaneously present the identification of the oppositions of actions (step 2) and the study of the convictions expressed by their opposed subjects (step 3) and by the opposed effects of the actions upon receivers (step 4).

8. This is the first opposition of actions. It is not possible to conclude that there is an opposition between "hiding" and "revealing" in 10:21: both are positive actions (they have the same subject, God).

who is in a special relationship with Jesus, a Father-Son relationship, knows who the Son is. Thus the text underscores that this relationship is a part of what makes it possible for the Father to know the Son; this relationship either establishes his will or enables him.[9]

OPP 10:22b. The opposition between those who know and those who do not know who the Father is contrasts two positive subjects (the Son and any one to whom the Son chooses to reveal him) with an indefinite negative subject (no one).

By contrast with anybody else (no one), Jesus knows who the Father is and also what the Father does (hiding things from the wise and understanding and revealing them to babes, 10:21), because he participates in the Father-Son relationship. Thus, as in the preceding opposition, this relationship makes it possible for Jesus to know the Father. From the description of Jesus as rejoicing in the Holy Spirit (presumably, the Spirit of the Father) and saying, "I thank thee, Father" (10:21), we can say that it is an intimate relationship.

Jesus further describes himself by saying, "All things have been delivered to me by my Father" (10:22). There is much debate regarding whether this phrase means that the Father revealed all things to Jesus or gave him power-authority over all things (since "delivered" means "entrusted").[10] By following the principles of steps 3 and 4 of a structural exegesis we can clarify this debate. First, whatever might be the specific meaning of this phrase, it describes qualifications of the subject Jesus (step 3); that the Father delivered all things to him expresses once again the close relationship between Father and Son ("my Father") that makes it possible for Jesus to know the Father. Second, the correlation of the positive subjects of the two first oppositions appears. As their close relationship makes it possible for the Father to know the Son, so this relationship makes it possible for the Son to know the Father. The rest of 10:22 expresses this correlation. As the Father reveals things to the babes, and this was his gracious will (10:21), so Jesus has been entrusted with the task and authority of revealing certain things to whom he wants (10:22). Thus the text underscores that the close relationship between Father and Son means in part that the Son has a task (vocation) and authority that

9. In OPP 10:22a and 10:22b we do not find any ground to decide whether this relationship establishes the will or the ability of the subjects. OPP 10:23-24 will show that it is the ability. In Matt. 11:25-27, the same text and the same oppositions are found. But because Matthew sets them in a different context, these oppositions express that this relationship establishes the will of the subjects.

10. See, e.g., I. Howard Marshall, *The Gospel of Luke: A Commentary on the Greek Text* (Grand Rapids: Wm. B. Eerdmans, 1978), 435–38 (who emphasizes the revelation of knowledge), and his bibliography; and Josef Ernst, *Das Evangelium nach Lukas* (Regensburg: Verlag Friedrich Pustet, 1976), 341–42 (who argues for the transmission of power-authority).

are similar to those of the Father. As we examine the effects upon the receivers (step 4), we see that the text emphasizes that as the Father has knowledge of the Son, so Jesus has knowledge of the Father. This correlation shows that this knowledge is of the same kind, since it is mutual. It follows that this mutual knowledge is not to be viewed as a revealed knowledge, that is, a revealed piece of information (this would be nonsense in the case of the knowledge that the Father has of the Son), but rather the kind of knowledge resulting from close relationship and cooperation. Thus, we conclude that the phrase "all things have been delivered to me by my Father" (10:22) does not mean that the Father "revealed" all things to Jesus, but that he gave him power-authority over all things.

The opposition also contrasts people who know who the Father is with those who do not. It underscores that in order to know the Father, one must have received a revelation from the Son, and thus be like the babes who received certain revelations from the Father. This correlation raises questions regarding the nature of the revelation one needs to receive from the Son. The outcome of this revelation is clear; one knows who the Father is. Yet the nature of this revelation is as ambiguous as that of the revelation to the babes. Is it the direct transmission of knowledge (a piece of information) about the Father? Is it another kind of revelation that makes it possible for the receiver to know the Father? Although believers have a status quite different from that of Jesus, there is nevertheless a certain correlation between them; in some sense believers are like Jesus. Could it be that the revelation they receive is in some way similar to what makes it possible for Jesus to know the Father (his close relationship with the Father and receiving power-authority)? These verses (10:21-22) do not allow us to answer these questions; comparisons with the convictions underscored by other oppositions will allow us to answer them.

OPP 10:23-24. The disciples ("you") who see and hear are contrasted with the many prophets and kings who did not. Since the text underscores that the prophets and kings "wanted" to see and hear, it is clear that they do not lack the will, but rather the *ability* to see and hear, by contrast with the disciples who have this ability. The disciples (unlike the prophets and kings) are able to see and hear because they live in the time of Jesus. Being at the right time and place is essential for being able to see and hear. In addition, the text mentions that the disciples are "privately" with Jesus (10:23), that is, in close relationship with Jesus, a relationship brought about by Jesus himself ("turning to the disciples . . . privately").

This last observation becomes significant when we compare the disciples with the positive subjects of the preceding oppositions. The disciples are like those (indeed, they are some of those) to whom Jesus wants to reveal the Father (10:22). Note that certain people of Jesus' time are excluded. This makes clear that, in order to be able to see and hear and thus to be *able* to know the Father, it is necessary but not sufficient to be in Jesus' time. One of the additional conditions is to be in a close relationship with Jesus ("privately"). As the Father knows the Son, and the Son the Father, because they are in a close relationship, the disciples see and hear because they are in close relationship with Jesus. Thus, *being in a close relationship with (Jesus or the Father) as something that enables one to know, see, and hear* is part of the pattern that characterizes Luke's system of convictions.

Another feature of this pattern appears when we take into account the ultimate effect upon the receivers (step 4). Those who are in such a close relationship and who know, see, and hear are blessed. As the disciples are blessed (10:23, by contrast with the prophets and kings who are not), so Jesus rejoices (10:21).

This is all we can say. The text does not specify what the disciples see and hear, although it clearly concerns what happens during Jesus' ministry and teaching.[11] Since not all people in Jesus' time see and hear, we can say that "seeing and hearing" is a special kind of perception of what is in front of oneself. This special perception is one of the conditions for being blessed.

The Dialogue Between Jesus and a Lawyer (Luke 10:25-29 and 36-37)

In the verses that frame the parable and express the direct dialogue between Jesus and the lawyer, we find two oppositions of actions. Let us consider these oppositions before studying the parable.

OPP 10:25-26. The exchange between the lawyer and Jesus is a polemical dialogue, since the text notes that the lawyer wants to "put him to the test" (10:25). With an exchange exclusively made up of questions, we have to proceed carefully in our elucidation of the points (convictions) underscored by this opposition.

At face value, the lawyer's question expresses (1) that he does not know what he should do to inherit eternal life, and (2) that he expects Jesus to teach him what he does not know. Since the lawyer intends to put Jesus to the test, his use of the term "teacher" (10:25) is to be viewed as ironical; the lawyer does not expect that Jesus will be able to teach

---

11. The suggestions by commentators concerning what the disciples "see and hear" (e.g., see Marshall, *Luke*, 438-39), namely, eschatological fulfillments, deal with the expressions of convictions in terms of the views of the implied readers (step 6). We do not discuss these here, since we seek to elucidate Luke's convictions underscored by the oppositions.

him what to do to inherit eternal life. He might even pretend that he does not know what he should do.

Jesus' first question, "What is written in the law?" amounts to saying: You have what is necessary to know what you should do to inherit eternal life; you have the Law. The rebuke implied in Jesus' counterquestion appears: Do not pretend that you need me as your teacher! The Law that you, a lawyer, know so well provides you with the appropriate teaching. Thus the conviction underscored is that *the Law teaches what one should do to have eternal life (the ultimate blessing); one does not need Jesus to have this teaching.*

Comparing this conviction with those underscored by the preceding opposition, we find here a negative specification concerning what Jesus teaches the disciples: he does not teach what one should do to have eternal life. Such a teaching is available in the Law that the prophets and kings already had. But having and knowing this teaching is not sufficient to be called blessed (10:23-24) and to inherit eternal life (10:25). For this, one also needs to see and hear something that takes place in Jesus' time, and, as his next question suggests, one needs to receive another kind of teaching from Jesus.

Jesus asks a second question: How do you read? By this question, Jesus has turned the tables. Now, he is the one who is testing the lawyer. Does the lawyer know *how* to interpret the Law?[12] For the readers, the expectation is that the lawyer will fail this test, and that Jesus will teach him how to read, that is, how to interpret. At first our expectations as readers seem to be incorrect. The lawyer answers correctly ("You have answered right," 10:28) when he quotes Deut. 6:5 (the Shema) to which he adds Lev. 19:18. But, when he quotes the Law, he merely demonstrates that he knows "what is written in the law." He has *not* shown that he knows how to read or interpret it!

The conviction expressed here appears: *It is not enough to have the appropriate teaching (to know the Law); one also needs to know how to interpret the Law.* In view of the preceding oppositions, we can suspect that what Jesus teaches (reveals) is primarily how to interpret, and that by seeing and hearing the disciples show that they have been taught how to interpret.

OPP 10:28-29 and 37. This new exchange is polemical. Since the text underscores that the lawyer wants to justify himself, his new question (10:29) is an objection to Jesus' exhortation, "Do this, and you will live" (10:28), that is repeated in 10:37, "Go and do likewise."

---

12. Recent commentators usually do not notice the significance of "how" in the context of the polemical dialogue; they are looking for a context in early rabbinic practices. See Marshall, *Luke,* 442–43.

The point of this opposition is clear. By his question, "And who is my neighbor?" the lawyer shows that he does not know how to interpret the Law that he knows so well. By contrast, Jesus knows how to interpret the Law. Jesus actually teaches him how to interpret the Law; by the end of the story (10:37), the lawyer is able to say who is neighbor to whom, a response showing that he has also learned how to interpret not only Lev. 19:18 ("You shall love . . . your neighbor as yourself") but also, as we shall see, Deut. 6:5 ("You shall love the Lord your God").

Jesus taught the lawyer how to interpret the Law in two interrelated ways: by telling him the parable of the Good Samaritan, and, in the direct dialogue, by transforming his question.

After quoting the Law according to which one should love one's neighbor as oneself, the lawyer asks, "Who is *my* neighbor?" (10:29). Jesus asks, "Which of these three, do you think, proved neighbor to (of) the man who fell among robbers?" (10:36). These two questions involve opposed views of the relation between two persons (a person who loves and a person who is loved) expressed by the word "neighbor." Since this word expresses a relationship of *nearness* (or closeness), it can be visualized as the relation of the center point of a circle (one of the two persons) to a point within the space of the circle (the other person, who is "near" and thus "neighbor" to the first). For the lawyer, the person who should love ("I," the lawyer) is the static center point of the circle, and the person who should be loved has come into the circle and thus is "near," "neighbor." Consequently, the lawyer says, "*my* neighbor"; he is the center point from which is measured the nearness of other people, who are or are not "neighbors" to be loved according to their position vis-à-vis him. For Jesus, the person to be loved (the person in need, the wounded man) is the static center point of the circle, and the person who loves is the one who has come into the circle (the Samaritan), and thus is "near," "neighbor."[13] Consequently, Jesus speaks of the neighbor *to (of) the man* who fell among robbers. The relationship between the two persons is reversed.

The lawyer could not interpret the Law correctly, because he envisioned his relationship with others in the wrong way. Interpreting the Law correctly demands a new perception of one's relationship with others, or more precisely, a new perception of who initiates and establishes close relationships.

13. I designate the "neighbor" as the person "who loves" (rather than "who should love"), because being a neighbor to someone already involves loving; approaching the person in need and becoming a neighbor is showing mercy, as the lawyer expresses in his answer (10:37).

As we consider how the subjects and receivers of this opposition are compared to subjects and receivers of preceding oppositions, we first note that the lawyer as a negative subject is a person of understanding; he is like the "wise and understanding" (10:21); that is, like those who do not know who the Son is and who the Father is (10:22). According to the pattern of convictions, it now appears that things are hidden from such people, because they do not know how to interpret what they have (the Law, and "these things" [10:21] that are before them [10:23-24]). Conversely, the lawyer taught by Jesus (as described in 10:37) is like the babes, like those to whom Jesus reveals the Father, like the disciples who see and hear. It now appears that Jesus reveals the Father to people by *teaching them how to interpret* (and not by giving them a revealed piece of information). "These things" are not revealed to them in the sense that they were put in front of them for the first time; they already were in front of them. These things are revealed to people in the sense that they are enabled to see these things; that is, they are shown how to interpret them (while the wise and understanding are prevented from knowing how to interpret them, and thus for them these things are hidden). In this light, the disciples (10:23-24) are blessed for two reasons. They are blessed because things take place in front of them (in their time, by contrast with the time of the prophets and kings). But all this would be to no avail if these things were hidden from them (as they are from the wise and understanding), or if they did not know how to interpret them (as the lawyer). Thus they are also blessed because they are like the babes and the lawyer in 10:37; that is, because somehow they have been enabled to see and hear by Jesus who showed them how to see and hear, as he taught the lawyer how to read and interpret the Law (10:26).

The correlations of the positive subjects of the oppositions also shows that all these subjects—who know (who the Son is, who the Father is), who see and hear, and who interpret the Law correctly—are qualified in some way by their involvement in, or their view of, close relationships. From our study of OPP 10:28-29 and 37 it now appears that a "close relationship" (a neighbor relationship) is properly understood only when the person in need is viewed as the center point of a circle. The person bringing love enters this circle by becoming a neighbor of the person in need. In this light, we recognize that the same pattern of relationship is expressed in the preceding oppositions. The disciples (OPP 10:23-24) need to be in close relationship with Jesus (in his time and space) in order to be able to see and hear (unlike the prophets and kings). The disciples, who are "people in need" comparable to the wounded man, are in close relationship ("privately," 10:23) with Jesus, who is a neighbor to them as the Samaritan is to the wounded man. Who initiated this relationship?

The text expresses it clearly by the words "turning to the disciples . . . privately" (10:23). Jesus makes himself "neighbor" to the disciples. Similarly, in OPP 10:22b, people know who the Father is because they are enabled by Jesus from whom they receive a revelation; the words "to whom the Son chooses (or wants) to reveal" express that a close relationship has been established between the Son and these people and that it was initiated by the Son who makes himself a neighbor to them. Finally, the order of the statements in 10:22 suggests that the close relationship between the Father and the Son is initiated by the Father.

In sum, the pattern of the relationships between (1) the Father and the Son and (2) the Son/Jesus and those to whom he chooses to reveal the Father (among whom are the disciples) is the same pattern as that of the relationship between (3) a neighbor (such as the Samaritan) to a person in need (such as the wounded man). But in order to be blessed (and inherit eternal life), one cannot simply be a passive recipient of the benefits of this relationship (as the lawyer is a passive recipient of the Law that he knows well). One also needs to "do" (as Jesus emphasizes in 10:28, 37); that is, one needs to interpret what one has received (e.g., to interpret the Law) and to become an active participant in this pattern of relationship by becoming a neighbor to others. For this, one needs to know how to interpret, which is what Jesus teaches the lawyer by telling him a parable.

The Good Samaritan (Luke 10:30-35)[14]

Since the parable of the Good Samaritan is a complete narrative, we consider it by itself, before studying its role in the context of Luke 10:21-42.

Step 1. The theme of the parable. It is easily identified by comparing the first (10:30) and the last two verses (10:34-35). This is the story of a man who goes down from Jerusalem to Jericho, falls among robbers, is stripped, and beaten; by the end, his wounds are bound, he is taken care of, money is given to an innkeeper to take care of him, and he is at an inn. Three inverted parallelisms form the theme: (a) beaten up, taken care of; (b) belongings (including money) stolen, money given; (c) outside of society (in a place with outlaws, neither in Jerusalem nor in Jericho), in society (the inn).

Steps 2, 3, and 4. The first two inverted parallelisms form oppositions of actions. In addition, the actions of the priest and Levite are opposed

---

14. For a detailed interpretation of the parable of the Good Samaritan, see D. Patte, *The Religious Dimensions of Biblical Texts: Greimas's Structural Semiotics and Biblical Exegesis* (Society of Biblical Literature, Semeia Studies [Atlanta: Scholars Press, 1990]), chap. 2.

to the action of the Samaritan. Let us deal with these oppositions in the order of the positive actions.

OPP 10:31-33. The Samaritan went to the wounded man, while the priest and the Levite passed by on the other side. The text specifies that all of them saw the wounded man, and thus were aware of the man's situation. The priest and Levite are not differentiated from the Samaritan by a lack of knowledge. Two other qualifications oppose them: (a) one had compassion, the others did not; (b) one is a Samaritan (i.e., a heretic), the others are religious leaders, a priest and a Levite. What is involved in this latter distinction is further expressed by the way in which their respective travels are described. The travel of the priest, and likewise of the Levite (10:31-32), is well defined and oriented; they are "going down that road," and thus, like the man, going from Jerusalem to Jericho. Regarding the Samaritan, the text simply says: "as he journeyed." From where was he coming? Where was he going? This journeying without defined orientation is the figurative expression of what a heretic is. Truly religious people have a clear orientation to their life; they have a worthy purpose to their life. A priest and a Levite have lives devoted to the service of God. Nothing can distract them from this most worthy goal. They have a life as clearly oriented as their travel is, even when they go away from Jerusalem and the temple. By contrast, a heretic is a person who has rejected the true faith, and thus has no true commitment and purpose for his or her life. Consequently, a Samaritan has a life that lacks true orientation as much as his travel does. But precisely because he has no true commitment, no true goal for his journey, he is free to interrupt his journey, to go to the wounded man, and to take care of him.

The surprising conviction expressed by this opposition is that one needs to be a heretic in order to do the right thing, indeed, that which one must do to inherit eternal life (10:25). As long as one is committed to the service of God, as the priest and the Levite are, one cannot do so, and thus one will not inherit eternal life. In order to be a good Samaritan who loves one's neighbor as oneself, one needs to be a Samaritan, a heretic. This point is reinforced by the two other oppositions, which we can treat together.

OPP 10:30, 34-35. The robbers who strip and beat the man are opposed to the Samaritan who takes care of the man and gives money for the sake of the man, and to the innkeeper who also takes care of him. The contrast between the positive and negative subjects is clear. But the effect of this second opposition is to associate the priest and the Levite with the robbers. The devoted religious people become quasiaccomplices with the robbers who are antisocial people. Similarly, the innkeeper is associated with the

Samaritan. In other words, secular people who take care of others for money are also good persons, in contrast to robbers, and also to the priest and Levite.

The Parable in the Discourse Sub-Unit (Luke 10:25-37).   It remains for us to understand the parable in its immediate context as a part of the dialogue between Jesus and the lawyer. The question is, How does this brief discourse of Jesus transform the views/convictions of the lawyer? The procedure we need to follow is, therefore, similar to that of step 6, when we examine how an enunciator transforms the views/convictions of the implied readers (the enunciatee). Here our task is simplified by the presence of other parts of the dialogue (10:25-29, 36-37) that clearly express the ultimate effect of the discourse: The lawyer is taught how to interpret the Law; more specifically, his view of the neighbor relationship is radically changed. Telling the parable contributes to the achievement of this twofold transformation.

In the same way as in step 6 we seek to elucidate the views that the author expected the implied readers to have and so we first consider the views that, according to the text, Jesus expected the lawyer to have. The use of religious names such as "priest," "Levite," and "Samaritan" in a discourse addressed to a religious person such as the "lawyer" makes clear that these names are discursive figures designed to entice the lawyer to identify himself with certain characters. More specifically, the text presupposes that, as a person devoted to the study of the Law, the lawyer associated himself with priests and Levites; together they form the elite of a society under God; they are godly people who are fully devoted to the service of God. The lawyer, priests, and Levites ideally implement the first part of the summary of the Law that the lawyer quoted (and that he is confident he knows how to interpret, since he does not raise a question about it): "You shall love the Lord your God with all your heart, and with all your soul, and with all your strength, and with all your mind" (10:27, Deut. 6:5). Conversely, the lawyer had a negative view of heretics such as the Samaritan. Actually, from his point of view, heretics are even worse than robbers, since they dismiss the true service of God, while robbers are merely antisocial. Similarly, innkeepers and other people performing services for money are not much better than robbers. The text also presupposes that, for the lawyer, loving someone as oneself (cf. 10:27) and thus having compassion and showing mercy (10:37) are attitudes that fulfill the will of God. Against his other views, he is led to identify himself with the Samaritan. Then, he is confronted with a view of relationships in society that is the reverse of the one he started with. Indeed, according to the parable, heretics such as the Samaritan are to be viewed as the only ones in a position of doing the will of God, of showing mercy to the person in need; they are those who are godly people. Common secular people such as the innkeeper are not far behind; although they do so for money, they take care of others. Religious leaders such as the priest and the Levite are no better than robbers. Even worse, it is their devotion to God that prevents them from doing the will of God.

In the context of the dialogue between Jesus and the lawyer (10:25-37), this reversal of the view of all the relationships in society is parallel to the reversal of the neighbor relationship between persons who love and persons in need. Since hearing this parable brings the lawyer to envision the neighbor relationship correctly (cf. 10:37), we conclude that it taught him how to interpret the Law (10:26). In other words, a reversal of the view that the lawyer had of the relationships in society is necessary for interpreting the Law as it should be interpreted.

In which way is it necessary? Does he need to adopt the reversed view of relationships in society presented by the parable as the only possible view of these relationships (the view that alone is correct)? The text shows that this is not the case by the way in which he responds to Jesus in 10:37, a response that Jesus approves: "The one who showed mercy on him." By these words the lawyer expresses that he correctly recognized who proved neighbor to the man who fell among robbers, and thus that he now knows how to interpret the Law. Yet he does not use the name "Samaritan"; as commentators often observe, for him a Samaritan remains a despised heretic. [15] This means that he did not adopt the view of relationships in society presented by the parable as the only possible one. Nevertheless, his answer shows that he considered the view presented in the parable as plausible; that is, as a possibility among others. According to his earlier exclusive view of relationships in society, he would have looked for examples of godly behavior (loving God and loving one's neighbor as oneself) only among those whom he viewed as godly people (e.g., priests and Levites). But the parable made it possible for him to discover such an example of godly behavior in a Samaritan heretic. Indeed, the parable led him to envision the plausibility of a different view of the relationships in society. According to this view, godly behavior is found among heretics precisely because they are not totally devoted to a specific view of the service of God (i.e., to a specific interpretation of "You shall love the Lord your God"). Actually, after hearing the parable, the lawyer who was like the priest and the Levite is now like the Samaritan. Earlier, he had an exclusive view of society that oriented his search for an example

15. E.g., see Joachim Jeremias, *The Parables of Jesus* (New York: Charles Scribner's Sons, 1963), 205.

of godly behavior in a well-defined direction (toward religious leaders) comparable to the well-defined orientation of the travel of the priest and Levite. Now he has a *diversified* view of society that frees him to look for such an example anywhere in society, including among heretics, just as the Samaritan was free to approach the wounded man because his travel had no specific orientation. Simultaneously, because he has such a diversified view of relationships in society, the lawyer can no longer conceive of himself as having a stable place in society; consequently, he can no longer view himself as the static center point of the neighbor relationship. Thus he is free to interpret "you shall love your neighbor as yourself" as meaning that one needs to become a neighbor to persons in need.

When the role of the parable in the dialogue is perceived, one can recognize that the priest and the Levite, who are like the lawyer in 10:25-29, are also like "the wise and understanding" in 10:21; while the Samaritan, who is like the lawyer in 10:37, is also like the babes in 10:21. These additional correlations make it clear that the wise and understanding are people to whom things are hidden because they are not free to enter close relationships (to become a neighbor) due to their exclusive commitment to a certain service of God (as wise) and to their definite view of hierarchical relationships in society (as people of understanding). Furthermore, it appears that the wise and understanding do not know who the Father is because they are confident that they understand "You shall love the Lord your God." Like the lawyer, they do not recognize that they need to be taught how to interpret this commandment. By contrast, the babes are people to whom things are revealed and who know the Father, because they are free to enter close relationships (to become a neighbor) due to their lack of exclusive commitment (they are not wise; they do not have a definite understanding of the Law) and to their diversified view of hierarchical relationships in society (they do not have a definite understanding of these relationships). Finally, the Samaritan (by contrast with the priest and the Levite) knows how to interpret correctly the situation in front of him (he knows how to recognize the correct priorities), like the lawyer in 10:37 who knows how to interpret the Law, and like the disciples who really see and hear because they know how to interpret what is in front of them.

Martha and Mary (Luke 10:38-42)

OPP 10:39-40. There is a first opposition between Mary, who "sat at the Lord's feet and listened to his teaching" (the positive action, as the rest of the passage emphasizes), and Martha, who "was distracted [or, drawn away] with much serving." The contrast between the subjects underscores that Mary is sitting at the Lord's feet (note once again the close relationship), while Martha is drawn away (not in close relationship) because she is involved in much serving (the wrong attitude). The contrast between the receivers of these reflexive actions underscores that Mary receives Jesus' teaching, while Martha does not (as the translation "distracted" expresses). These points are reinforced by the second opposition. **OPP 10:40-41.** This polemical dialogue between Martha and Jesus further underscores the contrast between Mary's and Martha's attitudes. We do not learn much about Mary; we are simply told that she "has chosen the good portion"—that which is needed or necessary. But we learn why Martha's attitude is wrong; she chose the bad portion because she is "anxious and troubled about many things" which are not important (needed).

Martha's words (10:40) are noteworthy because they presuppose a wrong correlation between the characters of this new story (10:38-42) and those of the preceding passages. Martha believes that she is doing the right thing; she is serving, and thus taking care of the needs of Jesus (and the disciples), as the Samaritan took care of the wounded man; as Jesus charged the lawyer to "go and do likewise," he should charge Mary to help her serve. But this view contradicts the whole point of what precedes. Before going and doing like the Samaritan, the lawyer needed to become like the Samaritan; he needed to forgo his certitude of understanding what is the proper service of God, that is, his certitude of knowing how to interpret the Law; he needed to listen to Jesus. Thus, Martha is like the priest and the Levite. As they have a defined orientation for their travel, she has a defined line of action, because of her certitude of knowing what is good to do. As they fail to perceive what the situation before them demands from them, she fails to perceive that the presence of Jesus in her house offers her the opportunity to listen to Jesus by sitting at his feet (as a disciple)—the opportunity of entering into a close relationship with him. Thus she is also like the wise and understanding from whom things are hidden; she is deprived of Jesus' teaching. By contrast, Mary is like the babes and those who receive revelations from the Son, and she will not be deprived of this good portion (10:42), as things are not hidden from, but revealed to the babes (10:21).

STEP 5.
THE PATTERN OF
THE SYSTEM OF CONVICTIONS
EXPRESSED IN LUKE 10:21-42

As we took note of the correlations among the positive subjects of the oppositions, we elucidated the system of convictions expressed in

Luke 10:21-42. Now we need to summarize our findings, so as to make it easier to compare Luke's faith-pattern with the faith-pattern of other texts (e.g., the Gospel of John as discussed above).

The convictions we found belong to three categories: the divine, Jesus as mediator, and believers. Since the greater number of convictions are about believers (the babes, disciples, the lawyer in 10:37, the Samaritan, and Mary), we first seek to establish the hierarchy concerning this category.

Hierarchy of Convictions about Believers in Luke 10:21-42. "Do this, and you will live" (10:28). These words of Jesus in response to the lawyer's question concerning what he should "do to inherit eternal life" (10:25) simultaneously refers to the ultimate blessing, "eternal life," and to "doing" as a condition for obtaining this blessing. Since Jesus' words follow the lawyer's affirmation that, according to the Law, one should "love God" and "love one's neighbor" (10:27), we can anticipate that "doing this" refers to several stages of the hierarchy, rather than to a single one.

In the conclusion of his dialogue with the lawyer, Jesus said to him, "Go and do likewise" (10:37), i.e., go and do like the Samaritan, who became a neighbor to the wounded man (10:36) and took care of his needs. This is loving one's neighbor, an action that involves (a) having made oneself a neighbor to the person in need, (b) on the basis of a new knowledge-interpretation of the commandment of the Law, "You shall love . . . your neighbor as yourself" (10:27, Lev. 19:18).

A precondition (previous stage of the hierarchy) for "doing like the Samaritan" is "being like the Samaritan," who is a heretic without commitment to a definite view of the service of God, rather than being like the priest and Levite, who are religious leaders committed to a specific way of serving ("loving") God (see Opp. 10:31-33 and 10:30, 34-35). Therefore, "do this and you will live" (10:28) also involves (a) loving God in a certain way (a "good Samaritan's way," which is unspecified, except that it is not like the priest's and the Levite's way of loving God), (b) on the basis of a new knowledge-interpretation of the commandment, "You shall love the Lord your God . . ." (10:27, Deut. 6:5). Thus, before loving one's neighbor (doing something for others), one needs to love God (doing something for God); and in order to be in a position to do so correctly, one needs to have understood-interpreted the Law in a proper way. In sum, the end of the hierarchy can be provisionally viewed as including the following stages:

— Having a proper knowledge-interpretation of the Law, i.e., of what loving God and loving neighbor mean (10:37);

— "Doing" something for God; loving God in the proper way (undefined; serving God in a different way than the priest and Levite; 10:27, 31-32);

— "Doing" something for others; making oneself a neighbor to people in need, taking care of their needs (10:33-37);

— Inheriting eternal life (10:23, 28).

In order to progress in our elucidation of the hierarchy about believers, we need to note that "having a proper knowledge-interpretation of the Law (loving God and neighbor)" involves knowing "who one's neighbor is" (10:29), or more precisely, knowing-recognizing concrete situations of neighbor relationships (10:36-37). Thus, we can expect that this same stage of the hierarchy also involves knowing "who God is," and knowing-recognizing concrete situations in which God or God's will is manifested. Furthermore, we need to note that "having a proper knowledge-interpretation of the Law" is a specific instance of a more general conviction: having a proper knowledge-interpretation of *God-given things and of concrete situations*. This is the case: (a) of the babes who have revelations (including revelations of "who the Father is"), that is, who know what is hidden from "the wise and understanding" (10:21-22); (b) of the disciples who are blessed in that they see and hear (the significance of what is before them in the time of Jesus; 10:23-24).

Having such a proper knowledge-interpretation presupposes (previous stages of the hierarchy) that these things have been revealed to oneself by the Son (10:22). But, as is clear in the case of the lawyer (10:25-37), Jesus does not reveal things to people by simply transmitting to them pieces of information, but rather reveals by *teaching people how to interpret* what they have received from God (e.g., the Law) or the concrete situations in front of them. Thus, we can discern the previous stage of the hierarchy, which has two interrelated components. In order to have a proper knowledge-interpretation, (a) one needs to *know how to interpret* (the case of the lawyer in 10:36-37), and for this, (b) one needs to have been taught how to interpret by Jesus (what Jesus did by telling the parable of the Good Samaritan to the lawyer, 10:30-35).

In order to be taught by Jesus, one needs to be willing to listen to Jesus' teaching (as Mary is; 10:39), and/or to be in dialogue with Jesus (as the lawyer is; 10:25-37).

Listening to Jesus is only possible when one belongs to the right time, the time of Jesus. As is underscored by OPP. 10:23-24, the disciples can hear (Jesus' words), because they belong to the right time, the time of Jesus' ministry, by contrast with the prophets and the kings.

Living in the time of Jesus is not sufficient. Listening to Jesus is only possible when one is in a close relationship with Jesus, a relationship initiated by Jesus ("turning to the disciples he said privately," 10:23; see also, "he entered the village" of Martha and Mary, and "Martha received him into her house," 10:38).[16] In other words, Jesus makes himself a neighbor of those who need to be taught. Another precondition for this correct interpretation of situations and of God-given things with the help of Jesus' teaching is that people have something to interpret (as is underscored by 10:23-24; the prophets and kings could not "see and hear" what had not yet happened in their time). Thus, the first stage of the hierarchy about believers concerns people having a preliminary knowledge (a) of the Law (as the lawyer does, 10:27), and (b) of concrete present situations that involve divine manifestations (interventions in Jesus' ministry; manifestations of God's will). This is a preliminary knowledge of the Law and of these situations, in the sense that people do not yet know how to interpret them so as to recognize their true significance.

We now summarize the hierarchy of convictions about believers:

1. Having a preliminary knowledge (a) of the Law (given by God, 10:26-27); (b) of concrete situations (in one's present) involving divine manifestations (10:23-24);
2. Being in the proper time (the time of Jesus' ministry, 10:23-24);
3. Being in a close relationship with Jesus, a relationship initiated by Jesus (10:23, 38);
4. Being willing to listen to Jesus (10:39), being in dialogue with Jesus (10:25-37);
5. Being taught by Jesus how to interpret (10:30-37); knowing how to interpret (a) what one has (e.g., the Law) and (b) what is before oneself (10:26, 33, 36-37);
6. Having a proper knowledge-interpretation of God-given things and of concrete situations. Having a proper knowledge-interpretation of the Law, i.e., of what loving God and loving neighbor mean (10:37);
7. Doing something for God; loving God in the proper way (serving God in a different way than the priest and Levite, 10:27, 31-32; giving thanks to God, as Jesus did, 10:21);
8. Doing something for others; making oneself a neighbor to people in need, taking care of their needs (10:33-37);
9. Inheriting eternal life (10:23, 28).

This hierarchy shows that the central role of Jesus is to teach people how to interpret, read, see, hear (rather than providing direct revelations, i.e., revealed pieces of information) as the means of revealing who the

---

16. The text avoids saying that the lawyer came to Jesus; it simply says that the lawyer stood up (10:25); he was already in the presence of Jesus.

Father is (10:22; believers need to know the Father in order to know what to do). But for this, Jesus needs to come into a close relationship with people (10:23; to become their neighbor), something that he does because he has received this vocation and this authority from the Father (10:22), because he himself has a close relationship with God. Thus we find the following hierarchy of convictions about Jesus. The similarity in pattern of these two hierarchies is clear when I number these convictions with the corresponding numbers of the preceding hierarchy.

3. Jesus is in a close relationship with the Father (Father-Son relationship, 10:22).
4. [Jesus giving thanks to God, acknowledging his gracious will (10:21).]
5. Jesus receiving vocation and authority from the Father (10:22).
6. Jesus knowing who the Father is (10:22).
7. and 8. Jesus entering into a close relationship with the disciples (i.e., becoming a neighbor, 10:23) and fulfilling his vocation ("doing," teaching them how to interpret, know, read, see, and hear).

Finally, there are a few convictions about the divine expressed in 10:21-22. It is enough to list them, using the same conventions for the numbers:

3. God in a Father-Son relationship with Jesus (10:21-22).
6. The Father knows who the Son is (10:22).
7. The Father revealing things to the "babes"; delivering all things to the Son (10:21-22).

As the numbering in the last two hierarchies shows, the patterns of convictions concerning the mediator (Jesus) and God are quite similar to the pattern of convictions concerning believers. The Father-Son relationship is the kind of relationship that must be established between Jesus or God and people, so that these people might become believers. This relationship, which is not initiated by the would-be believers, involves receiving from Jesus or from God something they need; namely, knowing how to interpret. Thus, Jesus' vocation and the believers' vocation are alike; the believers' vocation is to "go and do likewise" (10:37); that is, not only like the Samaritan, but also like Jesus (and also like God). It is a matter of becoming a neighbor—of initiating and entering into a close relationship with people in need, and taking care of their need. Yet Jesus' vocation is different from the believers' in that, according to this discourse unit, he alone provides the "revelation" that people need; he teaches them how to know. He overcomes people's most central need, namely their inability to understand, see, hear. As they carry out their vocation, believers take care of other needs that people also have, here the concrete need of a wounded person (10:33-35). Yet since such acts of compassion are fulfilling God's will (the Law), we can suggest that they are gifts of God (stage 1, hierarchy of believers), that people will be able to recognize as such, if (or when) they know how to interpret their own situation (stage 6 of the hierarchy of believers). In other words, by carrying out their vocation believers put other people in the position of becoming believers, provided that they are taught by Jesus[17] how to interpret their present situation.

Other similarities between Jesus and the believers can then be noted. As Jesus receives authority and power from the Father, so believers listening to Jesus receive this know-how. As Jesus knows who the Father is and what the Father does (10:21), and consequently knows what he himself should do, so believers are blessed, know what the Father and Jesus do, and consequently know what they should do to inherit eternal life. What they should do is nothing else than what God or Jesus did for them originally, or what previous believers have done for them in the name of God or Jesus; namely, entering into a close relationship with people in need, becoming their neighbor.

Such are the main characteristics of the faith expressed in Luke 10:21-42. Although the study of the other discourse units of the Gospel of Luke and Acts would allow us to discover the many other convictions of Luke's system of convictions, we would find in these other discourse units the same basic faith-pattern, as we found the same pattern in two passages of the Gospel of John. By proceeding to step 6 of the structural exegesis we could study the specific features of Luke 10:21-42 by elucidating how Luke strives to convey such faith to specific implied readers—Luke's discoursive strategy and the figures that he constructs to express his faith in terms of the implied readers' views. But by themselves, the results of steps 1-5 of the exegesis open up another and quite significant exegetical possibility. Since we have elucidated basic characteristics of the faith-patterns of both Luke and John, we now are in a position to compare their faith-patterns.

---

17. Of course, one can anticipate that after Jesus' death and resurrection someone else (the Spirit? the disciples?) will have to play the role Jesus played during his ministry.

Conclusion

THE DIFFERENT FAITH-PATTERNS
OF NEW TESTAMENT TEXTS

The full significance of the hierarchies of convictions elucidated by our study of John 3:1-21 and 4:4-42 and of Luke 10:21-42 appears when we seek to understand basic characteristics of the faith of each of these Gospels. Actually, these characteristics are before us, since these hierarchies represent the faith-patterns that respectively characterize the Gospel of John and the Gospel of Luke[1] in their entirety.[2] Yet we do not perceive them as characteristics of these Gospels as long as we do not compare them. One cannot truly claim to know what characterizes a faith, as long as one cannot say in which ways it differs from other kinds of faith. Now that the hierarchies of convictions of two texts have been established, a precise comparison of their respective faith-patterns can readily be made.

A COMPARISON OF
JOHN'S AND LUKE'S FAITH-PATTERNS

The main similarities and differences between the faith-patterns of the Gospels of John and Luke appear as soon as we print side by side their respective hierarchies of convictions about believers. By printing them side by side, we do not suggest that the hierarchies of John and

---

1. We can anticipate that the hierarchies of Luke 10:21-42 represent the faith-pattern of the entire corpus of Luke's works, and thus also of the Acts of the Apostles.
2. These faith-patterns organize and thus shape not only the specific convictions expressed in the discourse units that were studied, but also the many other convictions expressed in the rest of these Gospels. Consequently, by identifying the hierarchies, we have elucidated basic characteristics of the faith expressed by each of these Gospels, even though we have merely identified a few of its convictions.

Luke represent the same faith-pattern (as the hierarchies of two units of the same Gospel do). Even though they have similarities, the faith-patterns of these two Gospels are not the same. John and Luke represent two different types of early Christian faith.

We choose to focus our attention of the hierarchies of convictions about believers, because here, as in most religious texts, they are the most comprehensive. More specifically, a hierarchy of convictions about believers is the locus where all the other categories of convictions intersect. We have noted that the most common categories concern convictions about (1) the divine, (2) a mediator,[3] (3) religious leaders, and (4) believers. As these categories of convictions intersect with the hierarchy of convictions about believers, they form clusters of convictions that are particularly significant as we compare the faith-patterns of different systems of convictions.

1. Convictions regarding the relationship of the divine with human beings (would-be believers and believers);
2. Convictions about the blessings brought about by the intervention of the mediator on behalf of would-be believers and believers, and convictions about the evil(s) that the mediator overcomes for their sake;[4]
3. Convictions about religious authority and the role of religious leaders for the sake of would-be believers and believers;
4. Convictions about the believers' vocation toward other people; the believers as persons who contribute to overcoming needs that other people have, and eventually to providing what these people need to become believers themselves.[5]

As we compare the hierarchies of convictions about believers of the Gospels of John and Luke, we shall focus our attention on these clusters of convictions or, more specifically, on those clusters that are expressed in the passages we studied. After taking note of the similarities and the main differences of the two hierarchies of convictions about believers, we shall consider the convictions about the blessings brought about by Jesus, and about the central human predicament that Jesus overcomes for the sake of would-be believers; convictions about Jesus as mediator, and convictions about the believers' vocations.

---

3. In Christian texts, the mediator is usually Jesus. In non-Christian texts, the role of the mediator might be fulfilled by a nonpersonal entity, such as Torah in Rabbinic Judaism, or a sacred place (e.g., a temple), or by a community or institution, as well as by a person (such as a priest).

4. As we noted, one can also establish a hierarchy of "evils."

5. This is the hierarchy of convictions about believers intersecting with itself. Often, such a hierarchy takes the form of a circle. The first stages of the hierarchy (becoming a believer) often involve a contribution from a preceding generation of believers, who are carrying out their vocation (one of the last stages of the hierarchy).

In the case of John, we integrate in a single hierarchy the hierarchies established on the basis of John 3:1-21 and of John 4:4-42—we have shown that they represent the same faith-pattern.

John's and Luke's Hierarchies of Convictions about Believers

JOHN

1. Having some truth and doing what is true (3:21), as the woman who shares Jesus' rejection of the Jewish prohibition of social and religious interactions; having received a believer's testimony about Jesus (4:29, 39). Having a preliminary knowledge; first level of believing: believing something about Jesus.

2. Being willing to come to Jesus, and interacting with him (3:19-21; 4:30); being in the presence of Jesus.

3. Having one's former deeds and their true character exposed (3:20; 4:17-18, 29, 39).

4. Believing in Jesus; second level of believing. Believing in Jesus (3:15; 4:39) = Knowing he is the "light" (3:19-21), as the "only Son" (3:18), as the Messiah or Christ (4:25-26), as the Savior of the world (4:42).

5. Believing in Jesus' message; third level of believing. Receiving (and thus having) a knowledge of earthly and heavenly things (3:12). Knowledge that "now" is the time of the Messiah (4:25-26), of the harvest (4:35), of salvation and judgment (3:18-19). Knowledge of God's nature (he is "spirit," 4:24), and of the will of God and thus of one's vocation (4:10-15, 31-34, 35-38).

LUKE

1. Having a preliminary knowledge (a) of the Law (given by God; 10:26-27); (b) of concrete situations (in one's present) involving divine manifestations (10:23-24).

2. Being in the proper time (the time of Jesus' ministry, 10:23-24).

3. Being in a close relationship with Jesus, a relationship initiated by Jesus (10:23, 38).

4. Being willing to listen to Jesus (10:39), being in dialogue with Jesus (10:25-37).

5. Being taught by Jesus how to interpret (10:30-37). Knowing how to interpret (a) what one has (e.g., the Law), and (b) what is before oneself (10:26, 33, 36-37).

121

6. Having one's vocation (will) as believers established; "worshiping God in spirit and in truth" (4:24); being "born of water of the Spirit" (3:5-8), having "living water welling up to eternal life" (4:14) by knowing how Jesus' own will is established (4:7-26).

6. Having a proper knowledge-interpretation of God-given things and of concrete situations. Having a proper knowledge-interpretation of the Law, i.e., of what loving God and loving neighbor mean (10:37).

7. Carrying out one's vocation. Harvesting as the woman did by her testimony (4:29, 39); bearing witness to what one has seen (cf. 3:10-12). This involves leaving Jesus, as well as forgoing one's pursuit of the satisfaction of physical needs (4:13-15, 31-34), so as to transmit one's firsthand knowledge to others.

7. Doing something for God. Loving God in the proper way (serving God in a different way than the priest and Levite, 10:27, 31-32; giving thanks to God as Jesus does, 10:21).

8. Doing something for others. Making oneself a neighbor to people in need, taking care of their needs (10:33-37).

8. Eternal life (3:15-16; 4:14, 36), seeing and entering the Kingdom (3:5), sharing the joy of the sower (4:36), being saved (3:17).

9. Inheriting eternal life (10:23, 28).

Similarities Between the Faith-Patterns of John and Luke

As we consider these two hierarchies, we first note the similarities between the faith-patterns of John and Luke. In both cases, would-be believers have a preliminary knowledge of some truth (stage 1 in both John and Luke); then, they need to be in the presence of Jesus or in a relationship with him (stages 2 and 3 in both John and Luke); their will to listen to Jesus is established (stage 4 in Luke), which in John is what believing in Jesus accomplishes (stage 4 in John); they receive a teaching from Jesus (stage 5 in both John and Luke); as a result, in John their vocation as believers is established as they worship in spirit and are born of the Spirit (stage 6 in John), and similarly in Luke, they have a proper knowledge of what they should do (stage 6 in Luke) and love God in the proper way (stage 7 in Luke); then they carry out their vocation (stage 7 in John; stage 7 and 8 in Luke); and in each case the ultimate blessing is eternal life (stage 8 in John and stage 9 in Luke).

The Main Differences Between the Faith-Patterns of John and Luke

But as we take note of these similarities, it is clear that, at several points, our attempt to bring together these two hierarchies of convictions is somewhat strained. The main difference concerns *what Jesus teaches.* In both cases, human beings lack proper knowledge concerning the concrete situations in which they are (earthly things) and concerning the divine and/or the divine will (heavenly things). In both cases, this lack of knowledge includes not recognizing divine manifestations in the present and not knowing the will of God that believers should carry out. But the ways in which believers obtain this knowledge are quite different.

In John, this knowledge is directly transmitted by Jesus. Human beings lack certain pieces of information concerning their present situation—the knowledge that "now" is the time of the Messiah (John 4:25-26), of the harvest (John 4:35), of salvation and judgment (John 3:18-19)—and concerning God's nature (that God is "spirit," John 4:24) and God's will (John 4:10-15, 31-38). It is only after receiving this knowledge (new information) that believers are in a position to "see" the spiritual dimension of their present, i.e., to recognize in present situations the activity of the Spirit (John 3:11) and to "*see* the kingdom of God" (John 3:3).

In Luke, this knowledge is indirectly transmitted by Jesus. The primary need of human beings is not so much for additional pieces of information, but for *knowing how to interpret* what they already have. Thus, rather than providing additional information about "earthly" and "heavenly things," Jesus tells a parable. He teaches people how to interpret what they already have received (such as the Law) and what is before them (Luke 10:26, 30-37).

Differences Concerning the Central Human Predicament

The end result of the two revelatory processes are similar: believers are in a position to interpret their present situations, to recognize divine manifestations in these situations, and to respond to these divine manifestations by carrying out their vocation. In both cases, Jesus makes it possible for people to interpret the present reality as a reality in which the divine (or the spiritual) plays an essential role and to discern the will of God. Yet, John and Luke envision in quite different ways the "evil" (human predicament) that prevents people from doing so and that Jesus as mediator overcomes.

In John, the central human predicament is a lack of information, a lack of knowledge, and not a lack of ability to interpret. When people have received additional knowledge-information about earthly things (e.g., "now" is the Messianic time) and about heavenly things (about the nature and the will of God), nothing prevents them from interpreting their present situations correctly; for instance, by recognizing the role of the Spirit in the believers' experience. In other words, people already know how to interpret, but lack pieces of information that would ensure that their interpretation of their situations is correct.

In Luke, the central human predicament is not knowing how to interpret, a lack of ability to know truly. Having all the knowledge-information that one needs—as the lawyer who knows the Law does in Luke 10:25-28—is useless as long as one does not know how to interpret this knowledge-information. It is only when one's way of looking at situations—one's way of perceiving the relationships among persons in society and between human beings and God—has been transformed that one is able to interpret this knowledge-information and these situations correctly. This is what Jesus achieves by teaching in parables, but also by his interactions with people (the disciples, Mary and Martha). It is in this sense that Jesus "reveals" who the Father is (Luke 10:22). Of course, in Luke as in John, having the appropriate knowledge-information is necessary. But in Luke the acquisition of this knowledge-information does not present any serious difficulty. This knowledge-information is readily available; the lawyer has it before his encounter with Jesus. We can expect that, unlike the lawyer, other people might need to receive such knowledge-information, and that in other circumstances Jesus himself or other people (such as the disciples) provide such a teaching. But this knowledge-information, even though it might include all that one needs to know, is merely a preliminary knowledge (stage 1 in Luke), because one truly knows it only when one interprets it correctly. Thus, the primary role of Jesus as mediator is to teach people how to interpret.

Differences Concerning the Convictions About Jesus

In view of this central characteristic of the faith-patterns in John and in Luke—overcoming a lack of knowledge-information in John, and overcoming a lack of knowing how to interpret in Luke—one can understand the differences found in their respective clusters of convictions concerning Jesus as mediator.

In John, Jesus needs to have the qualifications necessary for providing new knowledge-information about earthly *and heavenly* things. He is the only one qualified to provide true knowledge about heavenly things, because he is the only one who comes from heaven (John 3:13). Furthermore, the validity of his teaching is established by the fact that he has and demonstrates the proper credentials. He has an authority that is delegated by God himself; he is "sent" by God (3:16-17; 4:34). He is the "only Son of God" (3:18), the Messiah or Christ (4:26), the "light" (3:19), the "Savior of the world" (4:42); that is, Jesus is the one who can provide authoritative knowledge-information that people need. And he demonstrates it by showing that he has an extraordinary knowledge of what people did: he exposes their deeds (3:20-21); he tells the woman all that she did (4:18, 29, 39). This is a demonstration that he is the Son of God, the Messiah, the Light, and the Savior, because people can verify the truth of this revelation; they know their own deeds. And we can anticipate that his ascension (3:13) and crucifixion (being lifted up, 3:14) are further demonstrations of the validity of the knowledge-information he provided during his ministry.[6]

In Luke, Jesus needs to have the qualifications for teaching people how to interpret. We noted that this involves teaching people how to envision in a different way their relationships with other people (the neighbor relationship) and with God. Thus, the convictions about Jesus include that he initiates close relationships with people (e.g., Luke 10:23), and that he is in a similarly close relationship with his Father. By his close relationship with his Father and by initiating close relationships with people, Jesus exemplifies the vision of relationships with other people and God that one needs in order to know how to interpret the Law and concrete situations. We can, therefore, anticipate that in Luke the ministry of Jesus functions as the parable of the Good Samaritan does; it teaches how to interpret.[7]

Differences Concerning Convictions About the Believers' Vocation

In view of the central characteristic of the faith-patterns in John and in Luke—overcoming a lack of knowledge-information in John, and overcoming a lack of knowing how to interpret in Luke—one can also understand the differences found in their respective clusters of convictions concerning the believers' vocation.

In John, when one has received from Jesus the knowledge concerning God's nature and the role of the Spirit, one is in a position of "worshiping in spirit and in truth" and of being "born of water and the Spirit" (John 3:5), which involves benefiting from additional divine intervention. This involves having the will to carry out one's vocation established (cf. John 3:8). Since Jesus is the only one who can provide the true knowledge-information that people need, the believers' vocation is to bring people to Jesus by giving their testimony (John 4:39; cf. 3:11); that is, by telling

6. Although the passages we studied do not specify this part of the hierarchy of convictions about Jesus, we can expect that elsewhere in the Gospel these convictions will be expressed following the pattern expressed in John 3:1-21 and 4:4-42.

7. This suggestion is supported by the study of Luke 24:1-53 (available in Computer Assisted Lessons). As in Luke 10 the parable provides a key for understanding the Law, and the interpretation of the significance of the Law is the necessary context for understanding the parable (a twofold process), so in Luke 24, Jesus' cross and resurrection provide a key for understanding the Scriptures, and the interpretation of the significance of the Scriptures is the necessary context for understanding Jesus' cross and resurrection.

people how they have been convinced by Jesus that he is the Messiah, and thus that his teaching is true knowledge.

In Luke, when one has learned from Jesus how to interpret the Law and concrete situations by being led to envision one's relationships with other people and with God properly, one needs to act accordingly: "Go and do likewise" (Luke 10:37). As we noted, this involves doing both as the Samaritan did and also as Jesus did. This involves giving thanks to God (Luke 10:21), as the proper expression of one's love for God. This also includes becoming a neighbor to people in need, that is, approaching them (as the Samaritan did, rather than passing on the other side of the road, Luke 10:31-34, and as Jesus did by initiating close relationships, 10:23) and taking care of their needs (as the Samaritan took care of the physical needs of the wounded man, Luke 10:34-35, and as Jesus did by taking care of people's need for a teaching that would show them how to interpret). These observations show that, by carrying out their vocations, believers themselves exemplify how one should envision relationships with God and other people, as Jesus did. Their behavior plays the same role as the parable and duplicates or prolongs Jesus' own ministry; they contribute to teaching other people how to interpret by leading them to envision relationships with God and with other people in a new way. This "vision" that believers have received from Jesus and that they transmit to others is a kind of knowledge—a knowledge of what proper relationships are—but it is not a knowledge-information: it is a "knowing how to know." Indeed, as a result of this relationship, one "knows who the Father is" (cf. Luke 10:22), as in John. But in Luke this knowledge of God is the result of having being taught by Jesus or by believers how to interpret, rather than a result of directly receiving knowledge-information about God from Jesus.

RESULTS OF A STRUCTURAL EXEGESIS

The above comparison of John's and Luke's systems of convictions takes into account only a few of their respective convictions. But because their convictions about the human predicament and its overcoming by Jesus are directly reflected in their convictions about the vocation of believers, we can expect that they will be similarly reflected in other clusters of convictions. Even if we cannot yet perceive how these convictions about the central human predicament and its overcoming by Jesus shape convictions such as those about the divine, religious authority, and the community of believers, we can nevertheless agree that our comparison discloses the basic differences in the faith-patterns of John and Luke. Through their Gospels, they strive to convey different types of early

Christian faith. The same conclusion could be reached by comparing the faith-patterns of other New Testament writings.

A structural exegesis of Paul's letters[8] shows that Paul's faith is yet another type of early Christian faith. For him, the central human predicament is neither a lack of knowledge of the nature of God, nor a lack of knowing how to interpret (i.e., a lack of cognitive ability). Rather, for Paul, it is *a lack of ability*; people are in slavery to powers, such as the power of idols or demonic powers, that are of the same order as the power of death. Such powers cannot be overcome by cognitive means (such as knowledge of the nature of God, or knowing how to know). To overcome them demands powerful divine intervention. This is what God did in Jesus Christ and continues to do through the intervention of the resurrected Christ and the Spirit.

Similarly, a structural exegesis of the Gospel of Matthew[9] shows that Matthew's faith is different. For him, the central human predicament is *a lack of will*. Although people might know the nature of God and the will of God, and are able to do the will of God, they do not want to do it. This central predicament can only be overcome by showing people that doing the will of God is *good for them* (euphoric), and thus that God, who gives such commands, is a loving God, a merciful God, despite the authority. Thus the lack of will to do God's will is overcome by Jesus who is "God with us," manifesting the goodness of God among us, and teaching the goodness of God's will. This is far from a teaching of God's nature or from a teaching regarding how to interpret. Furthermore, for Matthew, as soon as one's will to do God's will is established, nothing prevents one (makes one unable) from doing the will of God (by contrast with Paul's cry: "I do not do the good I want, but the evil I do not want is what I do," Rom. 7:19).

These different types of Christian faith that structural exegeses of the various New Testament writings elucidate are clearly incompatible, in the sense that one cannot hold these different kinds of faith simultaneously. Such results might be puzzling for modern believers. Is not Scripture one, as God is one? Obviously, it has unity, in the sense that each of these types of faith is a faith in Jesus as the Christ. Yet when the early church gathered together the New Testament, in its wisdom it preserved *as canonical* a diversity of Christian faiths, rather than a single orthodox type

---

8. See Daniel Patte, *Paul's Faith and the Power of the Gospel: A Structural Introduction to the Pauline Letters* (Philadelphia: Fortress Press, 1983), esp. chap. 7.

9. See Daniel Patte, *The Gospel According to Matthew: A Structural Commentary on Matthew's Faith* (Philadelphia: Fortress Press, 1987).

of Christian faith. In so doing the early church demonstrated that it had learned the lesson that Jesus (according to Luke) taught by telling the parable of the Good Samaritan.

Annotated Select Bibliography

This bibliography lists the works that marked the parallel developments of structural and semiotic research and structural exegesis discussed in the Introduction. It first provides a map of landmarks in the field of structural and semiotic research. Then it lists the diverse applications of structural and semiotic theories in biblical studies, which can now be incorporated in one six-step exegetical method.

STRUCTURAL AND SEMIOTIC THEORIES

The following are pioneering works in linguistics, anthropology, and folkloric studies. They remain the basis of structural exegesis.

Ferdinand de Saussure, *Course in General Linguistics* (New York: McGraw-Hill, 1966). De Saussure's insights were developed by linguists such as **Louis Hjelmslev**, *Prolegomena to a Theory of Language* (Madison, Wis.: University of Wisconsin Press, 1961).

Claude Lévi-Strauss, *Structural Anthropology* (New York: Basic Books, 1963). This book contains theoretical proposals that Lévi-Strauss implemented in *The Elementary Structures of Kinship*, trans. J. H. Bell and J. R. von Sturmer (Boston: Beacon Press, 1969) and in his studies of myths, such as *The Raw and the Cooked*, trans. J. and D. Weightman (New York: Harper & Row, 1969), and *From Honey to Ashes*, trans. J. and D. Weightman (New York: Harper & Row, 1973).

Vladimir Propp, *Morphology of the Folktale*, trans. L. Scott (Austin: University of Texas Press, 1968).

On the basis of these pioneering works, theories of narrativity were developed, especially by **Claude Brémond**, *Logique du récit* (Paris: Seuil, 1970), and by **A. J. Greimas**, *Structural Semantics: An Attempt at a*

Method, trans. by D. McDowell, R. Schleifer, A. Velie (Lincoln, Neb.: University of Nebraska Press, 1983; French, 1966); his "Elements of a Narrative Grammar," trans. F. Nef, in *Diacritics* 7 (1977): 23–40 (French, 1969); and his "The Interpretation of Myth: Theory and Practice," in *Structural Analysis of Oral Tradition*, ed. P. Maranda and E. Köngäs Maranda (Philadelphia: University of Pennsylvania Press, 1971; French, 1966).

While the above theories gave rise to applications in literary studies (see **Robert Scholes,** *Structuralism in Literature: An Introduction* [New Haven, Conn.: Yale University Press, 1974]), the number of partial semiotic theories grew, and general theories or meta-theories were progressively elaborated.

A first group of semiotic theories takes as its starting point the question of the process of *communication by means of signs*. The most influential meta-theory of this kind is **Umberto Eco,** *A Theory of Semiotics* (Bloomington: Indiana University Press, 1976). Eco seeks to integrate the diverse semiotic theories (including those of the second group; see below) into a general theory of communication by means of signs. It is the kind of semiotic meta-theory adopted by most North American semioticians, as is clear from the titles of two of the many publications of **Thomas A. Sebeok**: *Contributions to the Doctrine of Signs* (Bloomington: Indiana University Press, 1976); and *The Sign and Its Masters* (Austin: University of Texas Press, 1979). Such an approach is popular in North America because it can find another basis in the work of a contemporary of de Saussure, the American philosopher **Charles S. Peirce,** *Collected Papers*, 2d ed., ed. C. Hartshorne and P. Weiss (Cambridge: Harvard University Press, 1960); and his *Semiotic and Significs*, ed. C. S. Hardwick (Bloomington: Indiana University Press, 1977).

A second group of semiotic theories focuses on the question of *the production of meaning through structures* that govern the interrelations of significant features. The development of a general semiotic theory in this perspective has been the actual goal of Greimas's research since *Structural Semantics* (French, 1966) and *Du sens* ("Concerning Meaning," 1970). At first, Greimas and his collaborators developed partial semiotic theories focused on specific dimensions of meaning, especially regarding narrative. It was only after the establishment of these partial theories that Greimas was able to formulate the meta-theory found in: **A. J. Greimas** and **J. Courtés,** *Semiotics and Language: An Analytical Dictionary*, trans. L. Crist, D. Patte, et al. (Bloomington: Indiana University Press, 1982; French, 1978), and in the second volume of this dictionary, A. J. Greimas and J. Courtés, ed. *Sémiotique: Dictionnaire raisonné de la théorie du langage*, 2 (Paris: Larousse, 1985).

For a comprehensive presentation of this meta-theory and of its implications for biblical studies, see **Daniel Patte**, *The Religious Dimensions of Biblical Texts: Greimas's Structural Semiotics and Biblical Exegesis,* Society of Biblical Literature, Semeia Studies (Atlanta: Scholars Press, 1990).

In these dictionaries, Greimas strives to integrate the diverse semiotic theories (including those of the first group, including Eco's) into a general theory of the production of meaning. This meta-theory makes room for, and shows the interrelations of, a wide range of semiotic and literary theoretical research projects focused on the question of the production of meaning, in addition to the works of Greimas's direct collaborators, known as the Paris Semiotic School (see **Jean Claude Coquet**, *L'école sémiotique de Paris* [Paris: PUF, 1983]). In his meta-theory Greimas seeks to account for the following works.

The Polish Semiotic School led by **Jerzy Pelč**, "Semantic Functions as Applied to the Analysis of the Concept of Metaphor," *Poetics/Poetika/ Poetyka* 1, ed. D. Davie et al. (The Hague: Mouton, 1961), 305–39; his "Meaning as an Instrument," *Semiotica* 3 [1971]: 1–20); and his *Studies in Functional Logical Semiotics of Natural Language* (The Hague: Mouton, 1971).

The Tartu Semiotic School led by **Yuri Lotman.** See his essays in *Soviet Semiotics: An Anthology,* ed. and trans. D. Lucid (Baltimore: Johns Hopkins University Press, 1977), 95–101, 119–35, 193–97, 213–21, 233–52.

Mikhail Bakhtin, *Problems of Dostoevsky's Poetics,* trans. R. W. Rotsel (Ann Arbor, Mich.: Ardis, 1973). On Bakhtin, see **Tzvetan Todorov,** *Mikhail Bakhtin: The Dialogical Principle* (Minneapolis: University of Minnesota Press, 1984).

Boris Uspensky, *A Poetics of Composition: The Structure of the Artistic Text and Typology of a Compositional Form,* trans. V. Zavarin and S. Wittig (Berkeley and Los Angeles: University of California Press, 1973).

The early work of **Roland Barthes**, such as *Writing Degree Zero* and *Elements of Semiology,* trans. A. Lavers and C. Smith (New York: Hill and Wang, 1968), and *Nouveaux Essais Critiques* (Paris: Seuil, 1970).

Greimas's meta-theory is best designated as a "structural semiotics," the designation given to this type of semiotic research by **Herman Parret**, in *Semiotics and Pragmatics: An Evaluative Comparison of Conceptual Frameworks* (Amsterdam and Philadelphia: John Benjamins, 1983). Many of the schools and scholars mentioned above avoid using the word "structural" as a designation of their theories and methodologies because they reject basic tenets of the proposals of Lévi-Strauss and the formalists (e.g.,

V. **Propp,** *Morphology of the Folktale,* trans. L. Scott [Bloomington: Indiana University Press, 1958]) with which the designation "structuralism" was originally associated. But the phrase "structural semiotics" makes it clear that this theory goes much beyond early structuralism, and that this semiotics should not be confused with the semiotic theories focused on the question of communication through signs.

STRUCTURAL EXEGESIS

A diversity of exegetical methods was developed out of these structural and semiotic theories. The following works use one or another of these methods in biblical studies.

Lévi-Strauss's proposals were used by **Edmund Leach,** *Genesis as Myth and Other Essays* (London: Cape, 1969); **Daniel Patte,** *What Is Structural Exegesis?* (Philadelphia: Fortress Press, 1976), chap. 4; **Daniel Patte and Aline Patte,** *Structural Exegesis: From Theory To Practice* (Philadelphia: Fortress Press, 1978); **Robert M. Polzin,** *Biblical Structuralism: Method and Subjectivity in the Study of Ancient Texts,* Semeia Supplements (Philadelphia: Fortress Press, 1977), see esp. 74–83, a study of Job; and more extensively by **Elizabeth Struthers Malbon** in " 'No Need to Have Any One Write'? A Structural Exegesis of 1 Thessalonians," *Semeia* 26 (1983): 57–83; and in her *Narrative Space and Mythic Meaning in Mark* (San Francisco: Harper & Row, 1986).

Greimas's theory about narrativity (which progressively became more and more comprehensive) was used by **Jean Calloud** (*Structural Analysis of Narrative: Temptation of Jesus in the Wilderness,* trans. D. Patte, Semeia Supplements (Philadelphia: Fortress Press, 1976); by **John Dominic Crossan** (e.g., "It is Written: A Structuralist Analysis of John 6," *Semeia* 26, [1983]: 3-21; *The Dark Interval: Towards a Theology of Story* [Sonoma, Calif.: Polebridge Press, 1988; 1975]); by **Dan Via** (e.g., *Kerygma and Comedy in the New Testament: A Structuralist Approach to Hermeneutic* [Philadelphia: Fortress Press, 1975], and his use of structural exegesis, among other approaches, in *The Ethics of Mark's Gospel in the Middle of Time* [Philadelphia: Fortress Press, 1985]); by **Daniel Patte,** *What Is Structural Exegesis?* chap. 3; by the **Group of Entrevernes,** *Signs and Parables: Semiotics and Gospel Texts,* trans. G. Phillips (Pittsburgh: Pickwick Press, 1978). This group is made up of the members of the CADIR (Centre pour l'Analyse du Discours Religieux, Catholic University of Lyon), who publish the journal *Sémiotique et Bible* (since 1975). All the essays in this journal are based on Greimas's semiotic theory. We could add numerous studies in French to this brief list of studies in English. Here we only mention the work of **Agnès Gueuret,** *L'Engendrement d'un*

Récit: L'Evangile de l'enfance selon Saint Luc, Lectio Divina 113 (Paris: Cerf, 1983), and **Louis Panier,** *Récit et commentaires de la tentation de Jésus au désert* (Paris: Cerf, 1984).

Greimas's theory about didactic discourse (as a generalization of his narrative theory) was also used in biblical exegesis by **Daniel Patte,** "Method for a Structural Exegesis of Didactic Discourses: Analysis of 1 Thessalonians," *Semeia* 26 (1983): 85–129; by **Jean Calloud** and **François Genuyt,** *La première épître de Pierre: analyse sémiotique* (Paris: Cerf, 1982); and by **Agnès Gueuret,** *La mise en discours. Recherches sémiotiques à propos de l'Evangile de Luc* (Paris: Cerf, 1987).

The overall semiotic theory of Greimas is used by **Hendrikus Boers** (*Neither on This Mountain Nor in Jerusalem: A Study of John 4*, Society of Biblical Literature, Monograph Series 35 [Atlanta: Scholars Press, 1988]). The first part of this book provides an excellent initiation to a more technical use of Greimas's semiotic theory for biblical exegesis, while the second part presents the contributions of the semiotic analysis to the exegesis of this text by comparing its results with other exegetical interpretations.

Other semiotic narrative theories are similarly used in exegesis. Thus, **Olivette Genest,** *Le Christ de la Passion: perspective structurale* (Montreal: Bellarmin; Paris: Desclée, 1978), proposes an interpretation of the Passion according to Mark using the narrative theory of Roland Barthes. In a different way, **Norman Petersen,** *Rediscovering Paul: Philemon and the Sociology of Paul's Narrative World* (Philadelphia: Fortress Press, 1985), studies the narrativity of Paul's letters on the basis of literary narrative theories closely related to semiotic theories. Bakhtin's theory concerning the dialogical character of texts is used in biblical exegesis by **Robert Polzin,** *Moses and the Deuteronomist: A Literary Study of the Deuteronomic History* (New York: Seabury Press, 1980).

To my knowledge, the semiotic theory of Y. Lotman, with its emphasis on the social dimensions of discourses, is not directly used in biblical exegesis; one can suspect that this is because sociological theories or political theories provide comparable models. Thus Petersen uses the sociology of knowledge theories of Berger, Luckmann, and Geertz in *Rediscovering Paul*. See **David Jobling,** *The Sense of Biblical Narrative: Three Structural Analyses in the Old Testament* (Sheffield, Eng.: JSOT Press, 1978); and his *The Sense of Biblical Narrative II: Structural Analyses in the Hebrew Bible* (Sheffield, Eng.: JSOT Press, 1986). Jobling moves progressively from the use of classical structural models to the use of political models, as will be even clearer in his forthcoming works.

The six-step method proposed in the present book incorporates main features of each of these exegetical methods by the very fact that it is based upon the meta-theory that Greimas proposed to subsume the partial structural and semiotic theories. It is used in two different ways in **Daniel Patte,** *Paul's Faith and the Power of the Gospel: A Structural Introduction to the Pauline Letters* (Philadelphia: Fortress Press, 1983); and his *The Gospel According to Matthew: A Structural Commentary on Matthew's Faith* (Philadelphia: Fortress Press, 1987).